JAGUAR CARS

1946 to 2008

A Pictorial History

Nigel Thorley

VELOCE

CONTENTS

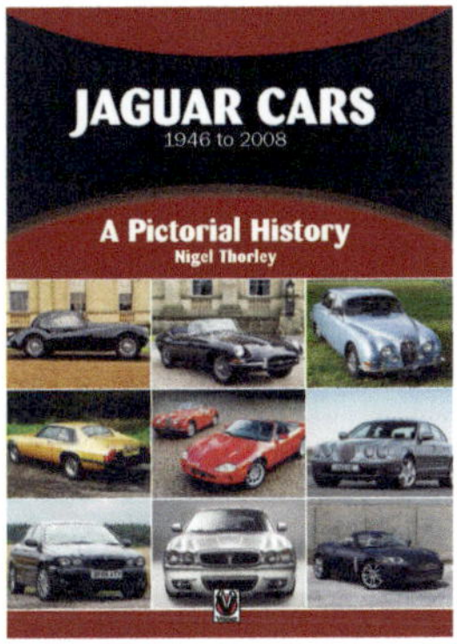
JAGUAR CARS
1946 to 2008
A Pictorial History
Nigel Thorley

A Pictorial History - more titles in this series:
Austin Cars 1948 to 1990 (Rowe)
Citroën Cars 1934 to 1986 (Parish)
Ford Cars – Ford UK cars 1945-1995 (Rowe)
Jaguar Cars 1946 to 2008 (Thorley)
Mercedes-Benz Cars 1947 to 2000 (Taylor)
Morris Cars 1948 to 1984 (Newell)
Riley & Wolseley Cars 1948 to 1975 (Rowe)
Rootes Cars of the 50s, 60s & 70s – Hillman, Humber, Singer, Sunbeam & Talbot (Rowe)
Rover Cars 1945 to 2005 (Taylor)
Triumph & Standard Cars 1945 to 1984 (Warrington)
Vauxhall Cars 1945 to 1995 (Alder)
Volvo Cars 1945 to 1985 (Alder)

Veloce's Essential Buyer's Guides:
Jaguar E-Type 3.8 & 4.2 litre (Crespin)
Jaguar E-Type V12 5.3 litre (Crespin)
Jaguar Mark 1 & 2 (All models including Daimler 2.5-litre V8) 1955 to 1969 (Thorley)
Jaguar New XK 2005-2014 (Thorley)
Jaguar S-Type – 1999 to 2007 (Thorley)
Jaguar X-Type – 2001 to 2009 (Thorley)
Jaguar XJ-S (Crespin)
Jaguar XJ6, XJ8 & XJR (Thorley)
Jaguar XK 120, 140 & 150 (Thorley)
Jaguar XK8 & XKR (1996-2005) (Thorley)
Jaguar/Daimler XJ 1994-2003 (Crespin)
Jaguar/Daimler XJ40 (Crespin)
Jaguar/Daimler XJ6, XJ12 & Sovereign (Crespin)

Other Jaguar titles:
Jaguar Mark 1 & 2 – Great Cars (Thorley
A Life in Car Design - Jaguar, Lotus, TVR (Winterbottom)
Jaguar from the shop floor (Martin & Starkey)
TWR's Le Mans-winning Jaguars (Starkey)

www.veloce.co.uk

First published in 2024 by Veloce, an imprint of David and Charles Limited. Tel +44 (0)1305 260068 / e-mail info@veloce.co.uk / web www.veloce.co.uk.
ISBN: 978-1-787117-76-1; UPC: 6-36847-01776-7
 Readers with ideas for automotive books, or books on other transport or related hobby subjects, are invited to write to the editorial director of Veloce at the above address. British Library Cataloguing in Publication Data – A catalogue record for this book is available from the British Library. Design and DTP by Veloce. Printed and bound in the UK by TJ Books, Padstow, Cornwall.

JAGUAR – A BRIEF HISTORY

Jaguar was born out of a business set up by William Lyons and William Walmsley in Blackpool in 1922, with the financial support of their fathers. Called the Swallow Sidecar Company, it designed and built motorcycle sidecars.

In 1926, Lyons purchased an Austin Seven chassis, onto which he incorporated a two-seater body. This led to the business diversifying into producing stylish bodies on existing manufacturers' chassis, predominantly the Austin Seven, but examples also included Morris, Standard, Swift and even Fiat.

The business name was changed to the Swallow Sidecar & Coachbuilding Company in 1926, emphasising the extension of work into body building. To meet demand, in 1928 it moved to a new location in Coventry (then the heart of the British motor industry), to gain access to skilled labour and a better supply of materials. Taking over an ex-WW2 shell-making facility in Foleshill, a natural progression came with the building of its own cars, creating a new brand 'SS'. In 1931 the first two models were announced, using modified chassis and drivetrains supplied by the Standard Motor Company.

The first of those cars, the SS1, utilised the Standard Sixteen side-valve six-cylinder engine and its smaller brother the SS2 based on the four-cylinder Standard Nine, both having stylish in-house designed two-door fixed-head coupé bodies. As Standard improved its designs, SS took advantage with additional models to attract a wider audience. Four-light two-door saloons and tourers were added to both models, and for the larger SS1 a drophead coupé and a particularly attractive Art Deco model was introduced.

During this period the Walmsley/Lyons partnership broke up, leaving the latter in full control of the business, which, at this time, still included the sidecar company, and a new company was formed (SS Cars Ltd) to look after the car division.

The next major change came in 1935 when SS Cars decided to further develop its models. Employing the renowned engineer

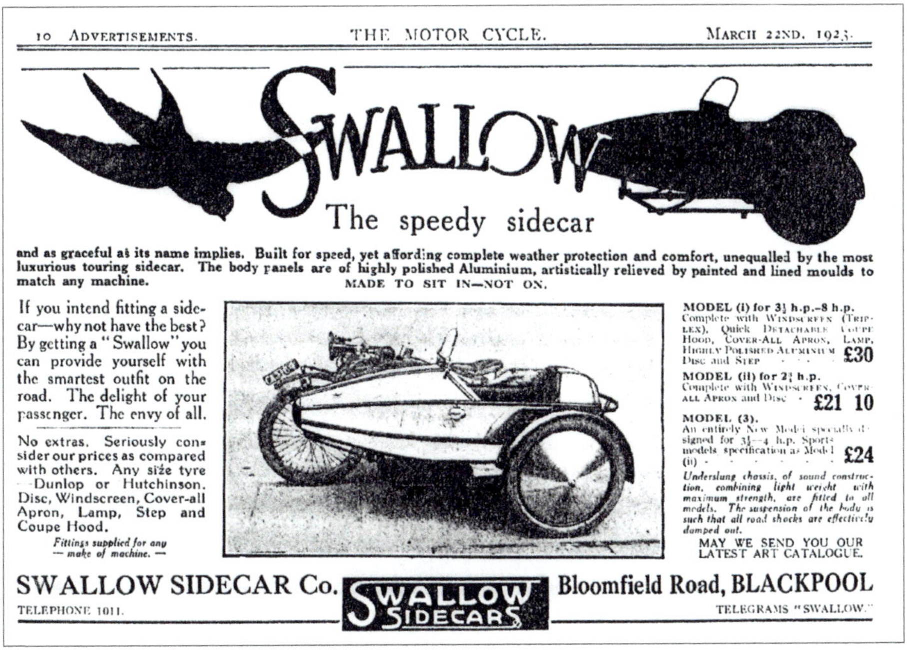

The start of the business, building attractive motorcycle sidecars in Blackpool.

Examples of the Swallow coachwork on contemporary chassis.

Harry Weslake, he reconfigured the engines to an overhead valve arrangement and Standard agreed to build them on the basis that the six-cylinder unit (now of 2.5 litres capacity) was purely for SS, while the smaller four-cylinder unit (1.5 litres) would be for SS but also available for some Standard models.

To complement the engines, SS had a new chassis designed along with an entirely new four-door saloon body, built using traditional aluminium and steel panels grafted on to an ash wooden framework.

Researching a name for the new car, William Lyons chose 'Jaguar', but he had to apply for permission to use it, as another Coventry-based car manufacturer, Armstrong Siddeley, already had the rights to the name, relating to its aviation side of the business. Fortunately they came to an agreement, and the first two SS Jaguars were born (although 'Jaguar' was then purely a model name).

As a means of creating further interest in the brand and emphasising the sporting nature of the cars, a few two-seater sports cars were produced: initially the SS90 with a version of the old Standard six-cylinder unit, and later the SS100 with the Weslake OHV engine.

These new saloons were joined by equivalent two-door drophead coupés. The whole range was highly successful, putting the company well and truly on the map of car manufacturers, but the outbreak of the Second World War meant turning the

The Swallow became one of the most attractive coach-built versions of the Austin Swallow during the 1920s and early 1930s.

An early example of the SS2 (circa 1931), the smaller model of the six-cylinder SS1 shown below.

The later redesigned SS1 six-cylinder model with flowing wings and extended wheelbase, circa 1933.

business over to production for the war effort – everything from miscellaneous items like fuel tanks to two-wheeled trailers, with the major production of sidecars for the army and even the refurbishment of Whitley bombers.

Postwar, as the SS insignia had very different connotations in the world, the name Jaguar came to the fore as the 'new' brand, and the company Jaguar Cars Ltd was born, which is where this book picks up the story.

Initially, the prewar saloons were reintroduced with just minor changes, although

Arguably the prettiest of all the pre-Jaguar SS models: the Airline.

the engineers had been working on other developments, creating a new chassis with independent front suspension and an entirely new engine, designed and built in-house. Both these elements were for a new luxury saloon, which, due to the extensive tooling for the bodyshell, would not be introduced until 1950.

As a transition from the old to new, in 1948 Jaguar introduced the Mark V saloon and drophead coupé using the new chassis, matched to a redesigned – if traditional – body style and the larger pushrod engines. At the same time, Jaguar introduced its new XK engine in what was initially planned as a showcase, low production two-seater sports cars, the XK120 (with the intended option of a smaller 2-litre engined version, which never got produced). All this coincided with a factory move from Foleshill to an ex-wartime shadow facility nearby in Allesley.

By 1950, full-scale production of the XK120 took place, and in the same year the new saloon, the Jaguar Mark VII, was introduced, a car that came to epitomise the company's advertising slogan – "Grace ... Space ... and Pace." It brought together the new chassis, the XK engine and an all-enveloping stylish body, a car that one American journalist called, "The prima ballerina of the British motor industry."

The 1950s saw significant growth for Jaguar, as the Mark VII and XK120 found success in sales and competition, with both models competing in racing and rallying. Using the new XK engine, specific competition models (the C-Type and D-Type) found success in international racing, not least at the famed 24-hour Le Mans.

During the 1950s, the XK120 sports car developed into the XK140 and XK150 while the Mark VII received similar upgrades to become the Mark VIII and later Mark IX. In the mid-1950s Jaguar introduced an additional smaller saloon, which also became successful in racing and rallying.

In 1956, due to Jaguar's success, particularly in overseas markets, William Lyons was knighted for his work for the British motor industry. Jaguar achievements in competition over that decade would result in a legendary reputation that still lives on today.

In the 1960s, Jaguar not only expanded its range of cars, but also acquired other businesses, like Coventry Climax (maker of a

The SS Jaguar 100, the first true sportscar produced by the company.

variety of products from Formula One engines to fork trucks), Henry Meadows (engine/pump manufacturer) and Britain's oldest vehicle manufacturer, Daimler. Its factory in Radford, only two miles from Jaguar's own facility in Allesley, allowed it to expand production, moving the assembly of all engines and transmissions there.

Within a couple of years the range of cars had been completely revamped, with the Mark 2 saloons (replacing the previous small model, only later known as the Mark 1), the Mark X (replacing the Mark IX) and the E-Type sports car (replacing the XK). In 1962 the first new Daimler model was introduced, the 2.5-litre V8 utilising the architecture of Jaguar's Mark 2 but with Daimler's Edward Turner (of Triumph motorcycle fame) designed V8 engine.

In the mid-1960s the marque continued to develop, with extra models, not least additional saloons, the S-Type and 420, increasing Jaguar's target audience.

In 1966, an agreement was reached to merge Jaguar Cars Ltd with the British Motor Corporation (BMC) to form British Motor Holdings (BMH), but within two years the British government wanted to bring the majority of the British motor industry into one group, so BMH became part of British Leyland, along with Triumph, Rover, Alvis and allied supply companies.

In September 1968, Jaguar made the decision to drop all the existing saloons and replace them with one new 'global' model, the XJ6. At the same time, a new Daimler DS420 limousine for the carriage trade was introduced to replace the group's ageing Daimler Majestic Major and Princess Vanden Plas. The new Daimler used the underpinnings of the Jaguar Mark X.

Despite being part of the massive BL conglomerate, Jaguar retained much of its independence. The XJ in various forms sold in ever-increasing numbers, and Jaguar introduced its second in-house designed engine, the 5.3-litre V12 unit, first fitted to the E-Type sports car and later to the XJ saloon.

In September 1975, the all-new XJ-S, 2+2-seater grand tourer was introduced, replacing the E-Type. Designed by Malcolm Sayer, the renowned aerodynamicist, this model would stay in production for 21 years in various forms.

Jaguar took control of the ex-Pressed

The luxurious SS Jaguar 2.5-litre four-door saloon, the first car to carry the 'Jaguar' name as a model (as 'SS' remained the brand at this time), this car also featuring the new Weslake designed overhead valve engine.

Steel-Fisher body plant in Castle Bromwich, Birmingham in 1977. Bodies for the range were produced there, and it later expanded to car assembly. In 1985, further expansion involved taking over the ex-Rootes/Chrysler engineering facility in Whitley, Coventry where future design and styling would take place.

Jaguar returned to successful racing in the 1970s and 1980s in various forms, culminating in another successful attempt at Le Mans.

The company gained its independence from BL, was privatised in 1984, and although the following few years were very good, the business still needed an influx of investment, finally being purchased by the Ford Motor Company in 1990.

A new engine, the AJ6 multi-valve six-cylinder unit, was announced in the mid-80s, initially fitted to the XJ-S but later replacing the XK unit in the saloons. In 1996, a V8 engine of advanced design (AJ-V8) was introduced, first in the XK8 (the replacement for the XJS) and later in the saloons. A year later, the V8 also displaced the then-ageing V12 engine. At the same time, Jaguar vacated the Radford (ex-Daimler) factory.

Although the big XJ saloons in various forms continued to sell into the 1990s, in order to keep abreast of ever-increasing competition from other marques like Mercedes and BMW, the range of models needed to be expanded. This came to fruition in 1999 with the introduction of the S-Type medium-sized four-door saloon (reintroducing the 'S' designation from the 1960s). With the V8 engine and new V6 units, the model saw Jaguar return to smaller, more economical models like the Mark 2 from the 1960s, therefore expanding its market share.

Yet another model was announced in 2001, the X-Type small saloon, creating a Jaguar competitive with BMW's 3 Series. Using much Ford technology, this model was manufactured at the ex-Ford plant on Merseyside. The range of engines included six-

and four-cylinder petrol and diesel units, and for the first time in Jaguar's production history, an estate car.

In 2003, Jaguar introduced lightweight aluminium construction for its bodies, which started with the next generation of XJ. A new 2.7-litre V6 diesel engine was designed in cooperation with Citroën/Peugeot, and over the coming years a whole new range of highly efficient engines came about, from 2.0-litre 'Ingenium' petrol/diesel units, to 5.0-litre V8 petrols and a new 3.0-litre V6 diesel.

Jaguar opened a new high-tech engine building facility in Wolverhampton, which would also develop the next area of propulsion: all-electric.

In 2006, the XK sports car range was redesigned (now with an aluminium body). A year later a new coupé-styled medium-sized four-door saloon, the XF, replaced the S-Type and X-Types, and in 2009 another new XJ was launched.

A year earlier in 2008, the Ford Motor Company sold Jaguar and Land Rover to the Indian Tata Group, which started the amalgamation of engineering and development of the two brands with facilities at Gaydon in the West Midlands.

In 2013, Jaguar introduced its new F-TYPE two-seater sports car, replacing the 2+2 XK, and in 2015 a new small saloon, the XE, was introduced, followed a year later by a revised XF, of a similar body style. That year, Jaguar moved into another market sector Sports Utility Vehicles (SUV) with the F-PACE and in 2018 a smaller E-PACE version.

Jaguar progressed by introducing its first all-electric vehicle, the I-PACE, and later PHEV and MHEV hybrid versions of some of the smaller-engined models.

The final XJ left production in 2019, not to be replaced, and all other existing ICE (internal combustion engined) cars were phased out during 2023/2024 in readiness for a new all-electric range, not covered within this publication.

MARK IV/V

In 1938 the SS Jaguar saloon bodies were re-engineered to all-steel construction, then in three engine sizes: 1.75 litres, 2.5 litres and 3.5 litres, along with accompanying drophead coupés. These models were reintroduced after the war, essentially the same with some minor changes to trim and specification. Retrospectively, these cars have become unofficially known as 'Mark IVs', to differentiate them from the later models discussed below.

A major change was the adoption of 'Jaguar' (Jaguar Cars Limited now formed) as the brand with no further use of the 'SS' insignia, for obvious reasons. The prewar SS100 sports car was not resurrected.

The only obvious change externally was the fitting of much thinner chrome side trims along the body. 'SS' badging was replaced with 'Jaguar' on the wheel spinners, 'J' on the rear bumper bar and a new style winged radiator badge with 'Jaguar'. The radiator grille was very slightly different in style as were the prominent P100 headlamps. There were a few mechanical upgrades but nothing significant, apart from the change of braking system to Girling.

Internally, pleated upholstery was now the norm (previously plain) and the omission of occasion tables in the rear of the front seats (previously only fitted in the late 1930s) was a cost saving. To cater for the export market, these postwar models became available with the option of left-hand-drive.

The 'new' Jaguar company needed to maintain sales during the development of an entirely new car, which wouldn't become available until 1950. Because of this, an interim model was released in 1948: the Mark V. Offered as both a four-door saloon and two-door drophead coupé, this car was only fitted with the six-cylinder pushrod engine (now manufactured in-house), featuring the new independent front suspension chassis

The only major body difference between the Mark IVs was the chassis length to accommodate the engines, in this case the shortened bonnet area for the four-cylinder engine …

… compared to the longer bonnet for the 2.5/3.5-litre engines.

destined for the 1950 model. With smaller, wider wheels, and, for the first time, hydraulic brakes, apart from some other minor mechanical aspects, the Mark V was very much the same as the earlier cars.

The body of the Mark V was entirely new with not a single panel interchangeable with the older cars. It was instantly identifiable by the substantial double-bumper bars, the flared-in headlamps and the more flowing lines with rear wheel covers (spats), making the model look even more streamlined. Other new

A typical example of the postwar Jaguar saloon, in this case a 3.5-litre engined version.

The radiator style was slightly squatter and wider than the prewar design. This is the frontal view of the 1.75-litre model with smaller headlamps.

The very stylish drophead coupé Mark IVs showing the revised postwar rear bumper bar with the prominent 'J' emblem in the centre.

The frontal view of the larger engine Mark IVs.

features for a Jaguar were the push-button door handles and the chromium-plated brass door window surrounds.

Internally the Mark V was also all new with a return to unpleated leather seating (as most of the prewar cars), and a redesigned dashboard.

NUMBERS PRODUCED: 1.75-litre Jaguar four-door saloons: 5761; 2.5-litre Jaguar four-door saloons: 1757; 2.5-litre Jaguar two-door drophead coupés: 104; 3.5-litre Jaguar four-door saloons: 3860; 3.5-litre Jaguar two-door drophead coupés: 560; 2.5-litre Jaguar Mark V

The Mark IV drophead coupés were not available with the smaller four-cylinder engine. The hood arrangement could be folded down completely as in the previous picture, or in the sedanca position as shown here.

All Mark IVs were fitted with wire wheels, usually to body paint finish or silver, but could be fitted with the optional extra Ace wheel trims, as seen here.

The comprehensively equipped dashboard of the Mark IVs. The badge on the top rail to the left, between the passenger wiper control and the handle to open the windscreen, is not original. Nor is the panel beneath the dashboard area.

The flowing lines of the Mark V, although looking similar to the prewar design, was totally different. Note the rear wheel covers (spats), the heavily chromed plated window surrounds and steel wheels were now a standard fit with chromed rimbellishers and hub caps carrying the 'Jaguar' name and inserts painted to match body colour.

The Mark V had a new style of radiator grille with flared in headlamps, auxiliary lighting and incredibly complex (13 components) bumper bars.

four-door saloons: 1661; 2.5-litre Jaguar Mark V two-door drophead coupés: 29; 3.5-litre Jaguar Mark V four-door saloons: 7831; 3.5-litre Jaguar Mark V two-door drophead coupés: 972.

PRICES WHEN NEW: 1.75-litre Jaguar four-door saloons: £684; 2.5-litre Jaguar four-door saloons: £889; 2.5-litre Jaguar two-door drophead coupés: £1189; 3.5-litre Jaguar four-door saloons: £991; 3.5-litre Jaguar two-door drophead coupés: £1263; 2.5-litre Jaguar Mark V four-door saloons: £1247; 2.5-litre Jaguar Mark V two-door drophead coupés: £1287; 3.5-litre Jaguar Mark V four-

A much more streamlined approach to rear end styling for the Mark V, including a covered fuel filler.

For the first time on a Jaguar (and most other British cars for that matter), Wilmot-Breedon push-button door handles.

door saloons: £1263; 3.5-litre Jaguar Mark V two-door drophead coupés: £1263.
COLOURS: Mark IV: Black, Ivory, Suede Green, Olive Green, Mountain Ash Green, Birch Grey, Battleship Grey, Lavender Grey, Gunmetal Grey, Dark Blue, Maroon, Honeysuckle; **Mark V:** Black, Ivory, Pastel Blue metallic, Pastel Green metallic, Suede Green, Battleship Grey, Birch Grey, Dove Grey, Gunmetal Grey, Lavender Grey.
TECHNICAL: Engines: 1.75-litre: size: 1776cc; cylinders: four; carb: single SU; bore & stroke: 73mm x 106mm; BHP: 65@4600rpm.
2.5-litre: size: 2663cc; cylinders: six; carb: Twin SU; bore & stroke: 73mm x 106mm; BHP: 105@4600rpm.
3.5-litre: size: 3485cc; cylinders: six; carb: Twin SU; bore & stroke: 82mm x 110mm; BHP: 125@4500.
Gearbox: 1.75-litre: four-speed manual, floor-mounted gear change; ratios: 1st 19.1; 2nd 11.8; 3rd 7.06; 4th 4.86.

The stylish drophead coupés continued during Mark V production, still very much hand-finished.

A return to unpleated upholstery for the Mark Vs.

A change of dashboard layout and instrument style for the Mark Vs.

2.5-litre: four-speed manual, floor mounted gear change; ratios: 1st 16.2; 2nd 9.50; 3rd 6.16; 4th 4.50.
3.5-litre: four-speed manual, floor mounted gear change; ratios: 1st 13.45; 2nd 7.9; 3rd 5.12; 4th 4.25.
Brakes: Girling rod operated drums all round.
Rear axle: Hypoid.
Suspension: Front beam axle, half elliptic leaf; rear live axle, half elliptic leaf.
Steering: Burman worm and nut.
Tyres: 1.75-litre: 5.25 x 18; 2.5/3.5-litre: 5.50 x 18.
DIMENSIONS: length: 1.75-litre: 14ft 5in, 2.5/3.5-litre: 15ft 6in; **width:** 1.75-litre: 5ft 5.5in, 2.5/3.5-litre: 5ft 6in; **height:** 1.75-litre: 5ft, 2.5/3.5-litre: 5ft 1in; **wheelbase:** 1.75-litre: 9ft 4.5in; 2.5/3.5-litre: 10ft; **track:** front: 1.75-litre: 4ft 4in, 2.5/3.5-litre: 4ft 6in; rear: 1.75-litre: 4ft 7in, 2.5/3.5-litre: 4ft 8in; **weight:** 1.75-litre: 26.5cwt, 2.5/35-litre: 32cwt.

XK120/140/150

The first postwar Jaguar sports car and the first vehicle to be fitted with its new six-cylinder twin camshaft XK engine, the XK120 was launched at the first British Motor Show after the war. A single production model in the form of a two-seater roadster with a hand-crafted aluminium body mated to a shortened version of Jaguar's new independent front suspension chassis, a chassis also launched in the new interim saloon, the Mark V, but ultimately destined for an entirely new saloon yet to be announced.

Due to the incredible response to the XK120 at the motor show, the company eventually had to gear up to full-scale steel body production by 1950 to meet demand.

The all-enveloping styling of the new car featured front wings flowing into the rear ones which were fitted with full covers (spats) for steel-wheeled models, without spats when specified with wire wheels. Exterior brightwork was kept to a minimum with a thin-ribbed split bumper bar at the front and just two vertical over-riders at the rear. Apart from the flared in headlamps and pod-mounted side lights, simple single lens rear lighting was accompanied by the combined reversing/ rear number plate illumination. A vertical oval radiator grille was mounted on a one-piece alligator-style bonnet.

Internally, split-bench type seating was fitted with full carpeting and a matching trimmed dashboard featured the comprehensive range of instrumentation with what was to become Jaguar's 'signature' four-spoke Bluemells steering wheel. Despite the comfortable interior, as was usual for sporting cars, there were no wind-down windows, just Perspex side screens, along with a detachable fabric hood.

The XK120 in its original roadster form. If fitted with steel wires, they were always painted to body colour and the now standard Jaguar chromed hub caps were finished with the centre sections also in body colour.

The unadorned frontal aspect of the XK120 with slimline split bumper bar. Note the side-light housing on the top of the wings, chromed on cars up to 1952.

A later XK120 with the side lights integrated into the front wings.

Although there were not many creature comforts in the XK120 roadster, all the instrumentation needed was there. No ashtrays, but a cigarette lighter was included! Note the now standard feature of all Jaguars: the four-spoke Bluemells steering wheel and the pronounced centre horn push.

After the move to all-steel body production, in 1951 Jaguar announced a second model to the XK120 range, a fixed-head coupé. This hardtop version used a separate bodyshell incorporating the steel roof beautifully sculptured at the rear like a saloon.

The hood arrangement on the roadster was rather crude, much like most other sports cars of the day.

The rear of the XK120 (in this case a fixed-head) with the simple rear lighting and bumper treatment.

The attractive fixed-head coupé XK120, in this case with wire wheels, at which time the rear wheel spats were not fitted.

The XK120 saw the first use of the new 3.4-litre twin-cam engine.

Internally the sports car was now a grand tourer with better trim, including a full wood veneer dashboard, wind-up glass windows and proper door locks and handles. A third model was announced late in 1953 with the introduction of the drophead coupé, combining the benefits of open-air motoring (with a more practical hood arrangement), plus the creature comforts of the fixed-head coupé.

In 1954 the XK120 was replaced by the XK140. Retaining much of the exterior styling of the earlier roadster and drophead coupé, the new models were instantly recognisable from the stronger deep bumper bars and the heavier cast radiator grille. The fixed-head coupé was even bolder, with a revised roof area incorporating larger rear side windows and longer, deeper doors. Internally there was more room and occasional rear seating for some models.

Mechanically, a revised chassis allowed the engine to be moved forward to create more room in the cockpit, and even occasional rear seating in the drophead and fixed-head coupés. A more powerful version of the XK engine was fitted along with rack and pinion steering. For the first time automatic transmission was now available on a sports car.

Only in production for three years, the XK140s were replaced by the XK150s in 1957. Stylistically, although retaining the overall concept of the earlier models, the XK150s had a new body with a more slab-sided approach, with a raised waistline from the front wing through to the rear. A wider bonnet with a revised grille, a one-piece curved windscreen, new rear boot/light treatment and a full-width rear bumper completed the external changes. However, the two-seater roadster was a much more civilised model than the XK120/140, in that it also incorporated wind-up windows

The XK120 drophead coupé offered the best of both worlds: an easily folded hood and interior creature comforts.

The well-appointed interior of the XK120 fixed-head/drophead with an abundance of wood veneer.

Showing the difference in door treatment for the drophead (foreground) and the roadster.

The revised frontal treatment for the XK140 with substantial bumper bar, new lighting and a cast radiator grille. The auxiliary spot/fog lights were an optional extra, but most cars had them fitted.

Revised rear end treatment for the XK140.

and conventional door locks/handles. Also the hood was of a better design and the rear styling around the boot and tonneau area made for a very attractive design with the hood down.

Internally, it was all new with revised seating, door panels and a completely new dashboard, now in padded trim, with no wood veneer available.

During the period the XK150 was in production, various engine choices (all based around the XK unit) were available, from the

The much more spacious XK140 fixed-head coupé.

Styling comparisons between the XK140 and XK120 fixed-head coupés.

Dashboard layout was virtually the same for the XK140 as 120, but note the flat steering wheel centre horn push.

The revised styling for the XK150 fixed-head coupé. Pre-1959 models had the smaller (red only) rear lights, while later models had the larger combined units with indicator lenses.

The XK150 drophead coupé.

The XK150 frontal view with wider grille, and note the one-piece curved windscreen.

standard 3.4-litre twin-carburettor model, through to the 3.8-litre triple carburettor version. As with the previous model the four-speed (with or without overdrive) Moss manual gearbox was fitted, or a Borg Warner three-speed automatic.

NUMBERS PRODUCED: XK120 roadster: 7614; XK120 fixed head coupé: 2680; XK120 drophead coupé: 1767; XK140 roadster: 3347; XK140 drophead coupé: 2790; XK140 fixed head coupé: 2798; XK150 roadster: 2264; XK150 drophead coupé: 2673; XK150 fixed head coupé: 4448.

PRICES WHEN NEW: XK120 roadster: £1273; XK120 fixed head coupé: £1694; XK120 drophead coupé: £1616; XK140 roadster: £1598; XK140 fixed head coupé:

Apart from the steering wheel, it was all new for the XK150 interior. The gearlever knob is not original in this instance.

Occasional rear seating was an extra touch for the XK140 and XK150 models.

The most powerful XKs were powered by a 3.8-litre version of the engine with triple SU carburettors.

Triple carburettor engine models carried this 'S' insignia on the doors.

Jaguar showcased its Le Mans race wins with an enamelled badge on the boot of the XK140/150 models.

£1616; XK140 drophead coupé: £1644; XK150 roadster: £1666; XK150 fixed head coupé: £17.

COLOURS: XK120: Bronze, Birch Grey, Suede Green, Black, Maroon, Red, Silver, Pastel Green, Cream; **XK140**: Black, Birch Grey, Pastel Green, Pearl Grey, Pacific Blue, British Racing Green, Dove Grey, Suede Green, Red, Lavender Grey, Battleship Grey, Cream, Pastel Blue, Maroon. **XK150**: Black, British Racing Green, Carmen Red, Claret, Cornish Grey, Cotswold Blue, Cream, Imperial Grey, Indigo Blue, Mist Grey, Pearl Grey, Sherwood Green, Imperial Maroon.

TECHNICAL: Engines: 3.4-litre: size: 3442cc; cylinders: six; carb: twin SU; bore & stroke: 83mm x 106mm; XK120:

The XK150 roadster was arguably the most attractive and practical of the XKs. This car came with steel wheels, which included full spats at the rear; very rare to see.

BHP: 160@5000rpm (std) 180@5300 (SE); XK140/150: BHP: 190@5500rpm (std) 210 @5750 (SE); XK150 'S': BHP: 250@5500rpm.
3.8-litre: size: 3781cc; cylinders: six; carb: twin or triple SU; bore & stroke: 87mm x 106mm; BHP: 220@5500 (std) 265@5500 (S).
Gearbox: 3.4-litre: four-speed manual, floor mounted gear change; ratios: 1st 12,29 (XK120) 11.95 (XK140) 12.08 (XK150); 2nd 7.22 (XK120) 7.01 (XK140) 7.16 (XK150); 3rd 4.98 (XK120) 4.83 (XK140) 4.98 (XK150); 4th XK120 5.64, 3.27, 3,92 or 4.30 (ENV), 4.09, 3.77, 3.54 or 3.27 (Salisbury), XK140/150 3.54, 4.09, 3.77 or 3.27.
3.8-litre: four-speed manual, floor mounted gear change; ratios: 1st 12.2; 2nd 7.16; 3rd 4.95; 4th 4.09, 3.54, 3.77 or 3.27.
Brakes: XK120/XK140: Lockheed hydraulic drums all round; XK150: Dunlop servo assisted discs all round.
Rear axle: Hypoid rear axle, Salisbury diff.
Suspension: front independent wishbone, torsion and anti-roll bar; rear semi elliptic springs.
Steering: XK120: Burman worm and nut. XK140/150: rack and pinion.
Tyres: 6.00 x 16.
DIMENSIONS: length: 14ft 5in XK120; 14ft 8in XK140; 14ft 9in XK150; **width:** 5ft 3in XK120; 5ft 4.5in XK140; 5ft 4.5in XK150; **height:** 4ft 4.5in XK120 rster; 4ft 5.5in XK120 dhc/fhc; 4ft 4.5in XK140 rster; 4ft 7in XK140 fhc; 4ft 5.5in XK140 dhc; 4ft 6in XK150 rster; 4ft 7in XK150 fhc/dhc; **wheelbase:** 8ft 6in; **track:** front: 4ft 3in XK120; 4ft 3.5in XK140/150; rear: 4ft 2in XK120; 4ft 3.5in XK140/150; **weight:** 26cwt XK120 rster; 27cwt XK120 fhc; 27.5cwt XK120 dhc; 28cwt XK140 rster; 28cwt XK140 fhc; 28 cwt XK140 dhcl; 28.75cwt XK150 rster; 29cwt XK1150 fhc/dhc.

MARK VII/VIII/IX

All the company's engineering developments during and immediately after the postwar period finally came to fruition with the introduction of the Mark VII saloon in 1950. Employing the new chassis (first seen in the Mark V) with the XK six-cylinder twin-cam engine, incorporated within a very stylish all-enveloping new body, the Mark VII offered customers a well-designed, high-performance and superb-handling saloon with all the interior refinements expected of a luxury car at the time.

Of all steel construction, with flowing integrated wings, a prominent (but very different) radiator grille) with jaguar head on the bonnet, ribbed bumper bars and full spats over the rear wheels, the whole design was very modern for its day, and certainly much smoother than anything else produced by other manufacturers.

Unique to the early Mark VIIs were the bumper bars, inset auxiliary fog lamps, radiator grille and badge/jaguar head mascot.

Internally, an extensive mix of leather and wood veneer featured with a well-stocked dashboard and creature comforts like height-adjustable front seats, and even an abundance of ashtrays!

In 1953, as well as having a manual four-speed Moss gearbox with or without overdrive, the car became available with a BorgWarner three-speed automatic transmission, and in 1954 the model was upgraded to the Mark VIIM with improved performance, exterior trim changes and interior enhancements.

In readiness for more significant changes, the model was again updated in 1956 and renamed the Mark VIII. Externally this model's bodywork was identical to the earlier cars but now featured a chromed swage line trim along the sides with the option of duotone paint schemes. The radiator grille was more prominent, sporting a Jaguar 'leaper' on the bonnet. Internally, seating and other trim was improved with the fitment of veneered occasional tables in the backs of the front

The Mark VII as it came out in 1950, with, in the background, the Mark IX, the final development of the style. Salient features are the unique radiator grille and mascot, the split-windscreen and rear-wheel spats.

Rear view of the early Mark VII with basic lighting and twin-handled boot locks.

Mark VII dashboard layout with the prominent top rail incorporating the rear-view mirror.

seats and an individualised rear seatback. For a while, the previous Mark VIIM remained available alongside the Mark VIII.

In 1958 the last variant of the design was introduced, the Mark IX. Looking exactly the same as the Mark VIII from the outside (except for badging on the boot lid) and virtually the same internally, mechanically the model was much improved. Using a larger 3.8-litre version of the XK engine (now developing 220bhp),

From the introduction of the Mark VIIM, the steering wheel lost the bulbous centre horn button (a feature from the XK120, see earlier chapter). Automatic transmission became available with this model, the control fitted as shown above the steering column.

Unique to the Mark VII to IX models were fitted tool kits in both front doors.

The Mark VIIM from 1954 with new deeper bumper bars, auxiliary lighting fitted separately to the front panel, separate indicators and inset horn grilles.

Visually identical to the later Mark IX, the Mark VIII featured side chromes, the choice of duotone paintwork and twin exhausts.

Mark VIII/IX frontal view, the only change from the Mark VIIM being the new radiator grille.

the car was also equipped with four-wheel disc brakes and power-assisted steering. Initially, this was on sale at the same time as the Mark VIII while stocks lasted!

Production of this range of cars finished in 1961, to make way for an entirely new flagship saloon, the Mark X.

NB: A few of these cars were specially prepared for military use, and known as the Mark VIIIB. They had de-tuned engines, and although with reduced trim, had a revised bench front-seat arrangement with a limousine-style centre-division to the rear compartment.

NUMBERS PRODUCED: Mark VII: 20,937; Mark VIIM: 10,060; Mark VII: 6247; Mark IX: 10.002.
PRICES WHEN NEW: Mark VII: £1276; Mark VIIM: £1680; Mark VIII: £1997; Mark IX: £1994.
COLOURS: Mark VII/VIIM: Suede Green, Ivory/Cream/Old English White, Birch Grey, Battleship Grey, Lavender Grey, Gunmetal, Black, Pastel Green, Pastel Blue, Dove Grey, Twilight Blue. British Racing Green, Maroon, Pearl Grey, Red, Indigo Blue; **Mark VIII:** Imperial Maroon, Claret, Cream, Sherwood Green, Pearl Grey, Cornish Grey, Mist Grey, Indigo Blue, Cotswold Blue, British Racing Green, Black; Duotones: Claret/Imperial

A late model Mark IX with revised rear lighting.

The modified dashboard for the Mark VIII/IX. The only difference between the VIII and IX being the indicator control switch, moved from the centre box of the steering wheel on the Mark VIII to a stalk on the Mark IX.

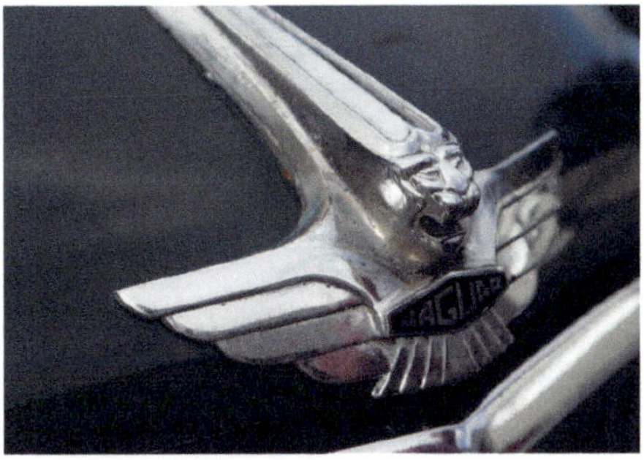

Mark VII/VIIM bonnet badge/mascot.

Mark VIII/IX bonnet badge/mascot.

The interior of a rare Mark VIIIB with centre division.

Maroon, Black/Claret, Black/Sherwood Green, Cornish/Mist Grey, Indigo/Cotswold, British Racing/Forest Green. **Mark IX**: Black, British Racing Green, Carmen Red, Claret, Cornish Grey, Mist Grey, Cotswold Blue, Old English White, Imperial Maroon, Indigo Blue, Pastel Blue, Pearl Grey, Sherwood Green; Duotones: Black/Sherwood Green, Black/Old English White, Black/Claret, Claret/Imperial Maroon, Cornish/Mist Grey, Indigo/Cotswold Blue.

TECHNICAL: **Engines:** 3.4-litre: Size: 3442cc; cylinders: six; carb: twin SU; bore & stroke: 83mm x 106mm; BHP: 160@5200 (Mark VII); 190@5500 (Mark VIIM); 210@5500 (Mark VIII).

3.8-litre: size: 3781cc; cylinders: six; carb: twin; bore & stroke: 87mm x 106mm; BHP: 220@5500.

Gearbox: 3.4-litre: four-speed manual, floor mounted gear change; ratios: 1st 12.73;

The different rear lighting treatment from early Mark VII (above left), through Mark VIIM/VIII/ early Mark IX (above), to post-1959 Mark IX.

2nd 7.47; 3rd 5.17; 4th 4.27; three-speed automatic, column mounted change; ratios: low 21.2 to 9.86; intermediate 13.2 to 6.14; top 4.27.
Brakes: Mark VII/VIIM/VIII: Girling hydraulic servo assisted drums all round; Mark IX: Dunlop hydraulic servo assisted discs all round.
Rear axle: live axle.
Suspension: front independent wishbone, torsion and anti-roll bar; rear half elliptic springs.
Steering: Mark VII/VIIM/VIII: Burman worm and nut; Mark IX: Burman with power assistance.
Tyres: 6.70 x 16.
DIMENSIONS: length: 16ft 4.5in; **width:** 6ft 1in; **height:** 5ft 3in; **wheelbase:** 10ft; **track:** front 4ft 8in (4ft 8.5in post 1952), rear 4ft 9.5in (4ft 10in post 1952); **weight:** 34.5cwt (Mark VII), 34.75cwt (Mark VIIM), 36cwt (Mark VIII), 35.5cwt (Mark IX).

MARK 1, 2, 240/340

Although Jaguar enjoyed great success in the 1950s with its large saloon and sports car, William Lyons wanted to capture a wider market: those who wanted a small luxury saloon with sports appeal. Work began as early as 1952 and finally came to fruition for the 1955 British Motor show, in a car called the 2.4-litre.

Using the now well-established XK six-cylinder engine, but in a new configuration of 2483cc, mated to the usual Moss four-speed gearbox, stylistically it resembled Jaguar's other models in many ways, both internally and externally. The big difference was that this was Jaguar's first monocoque (chassisless) vehicle, and its condensed measurements with good performance made it an attractive proposition; highly competitive against other comparable saloons of the period.

The purity of line of the original 2.4-litre saloon from 1956, with full rear wheel spats, tapering rear styling and metal window frames.

The stylish bodywork resembled elements of both its larger brother (Mark VII) and the XK sports car but in a smaller package that was instantly identifiably different, yet still looked like a Jaguar. A throwback to earlier days were the inclusive painted window frames with the door panel work, at the time thought necessary to ensure rigidity.

Internally, it was also very Jaguar but with yet another different dashboard, seating and other trim. Originally planned to run as a two-model range, the proposed 'Standard' model without a bonnet mascot, auxiliary lights, rev counter, etc, didn't enter production, so leaving just one model with manual transmission for the first year of production.

In February 1957 a second version became available utilising the 3.4-litre engine

The 2.4-litre frontal styling took cues from the contemporary XK sports car. The fog/spot lights were a standard fit on home market cars, the cast radiator grille applied only to the early examples.

The rear-end styling of the 2.4/3.4-litre cars echoed that of their big brother (Mark VII). This later car, fitted with wire wheels, has the cut-away rear spats, emphasising the narrower rear track of these models.

to increase performance, making the car more attractive to the valued US market. Trim changes included a new wider radiator grille to aid cooling, cut-away rear wheel spats and the introduction of disc brakes and automatic transmission (all features later adopted for the 2.4-litre model as well).

After a successful three years, Jaguar effectively revisited these compact saloons to create the Mark 2 in 1959 (the earlier cars became known as Mark 1s, even though they were never officially marketed as such).

Although at first glance looking remarkably similar, the differences were significant: revised lighting and grille at the front, new lighting treatment at the rear, a return to separate chrome plated window surrounds and a larger glass area, and a raised roof area. The rear track was also widened to improve handling and look more pleasing aesthetically.

Internally it was virtually all new, the only carry-overs being the window winders and door handles. The dashboard layout was to become a standard design feature for all subsequent Jaguars through the 1960s, with the speedometer and rev counter directly ahead of the driver and all other gauges and switchgear on a centre panel. A centre console contained the heater controls, radio, speaker and gearlever.

Mechanically, additional to the 2.4- and 3.4-litre engines, a high-performance 3.8-litre version was offered, this model making the car the fastest production saloon available at the time.

With Jaguar's acquisition of the Daimler Motor Company in 1960, by 1962 a 'Daimlerised' version of the Mark 2 was also available with a 2.5-litre V8 engine – not part of this publication on Jaguar models.

By 1967, Jaguar had an extensive range of saloons – along with the three Mark 2s plus the Daimler V8, there were two 'S' models and two 420s (both of the latter covered in a following chapter). Jaguar now needed to refine its saloon offering, slowly leading to the demise of all the existing cars with the introduction of the new XJ6 (see later chapter).

It started with the deletion of the 3.8-litre Mark 2 from the range, followed by the simplification of the 2.4- and 3.4-litre Mark 2s, now re-badged as '240' and '340'. To keep prices down, leather trim became an extra cost option, and the substantial bumper bars were replaced by a slimline type from the 'S' models. Another extra cost item was the fitting of the auxiliary spot/fog lights, now replaced by

The interior of the 2.4/3.4-litre models featured bucket front seating and a new dashboard layout.

A later 2.4-litre with the wider grille, standard steel wheels with conventional Jaguar hubcaps, and wheels in body colour.

When automatic transmission became available on the 3.4-litre car, different split-bench front seating was fitted.

A comparison of the original 2.4-litre (left) with a cast radiator grille and the later 2.4/3.4-litre models with a wider grille to aid engine cooling.

mock grilles. Despite the 'economy' measures, the inefficient Solex carburettors were replaced by SUs on the 2.4-litre engine, and the XK's cylinder head was now of the straight-port variety, providing better performance all round.

The last 340 left production in 1968 and the last 240 in 1969.

NUMBERS PRODUCED: 2.4-litre: 19,705; 3.4-litre: 27,280; 2.4-litre Mark 2: 26,322; 3.4-litre Mark 2: 29,531; 3.8-litre Mark 2: 27,848; 240: 4430; 340: 2804.

PRICES WHEN NEW:; 2.4-litre: £1344; 3.4-litre: £1672; 2.4-litre Mark 2: £1534; 3.4-litre Mark 2: £1669; 3.8-litre Mark 2: £1779; 240: £1365; 340: £1443.

COLOURS: 2.4/3.4-litre: Arbor Green, Battleship Grey, Birch Grey, Black, British Racing Green, Carmen Red, Cream, Dove Grey, Lavender Grey, Maroon, Pacific Blue, Pastel Blue, Pastel Green, Pearl Grey, Suede Green, Imperial Maroon, Claret, Sherwood Green, Cornish Grey, Mist Grey, Indigo Blue, Cotswold Blue; **Mark 2**: Cream, Old English White, Pearl Grey, Mist Grey, Cornish Grey, Cotswold Blue, Sherwood Green, Black, Carmen Red, Imperial Maroon, Claret, British Racing Green, Opalescent Silver Grey, Opalescent Gunmetal, Opalescent Silver Blue, Opalescent Blue, Opalescent Bronze, Opalescent Dark Green, Opalescent Maroon;

The extensively modified and enhanced design for the Mark 2 from 1959. Note the revised front end with another new radiator grille with a broad central bar, the flush-mounted fog/spot lights, and the conventional wing-mounted side lights and lower indicator lights following the practice of all other Jaguar models at the time. Also, note the chrome-plated brass window frames, instead of the metal type fitted to the earlier models.

This rear view of a Mark 2 shows the wider rear track, larger light units, and the 'disc brake' badge in the rear bumper bar.

240/340: Black, Beige, Carmen Red, Cream, Dark Blue, Willow Green, Warwick Grey, Ascot Fawn, Sable, Regency Red, British Racing Green, Light Blue.

TECHNICAL: **Engines:** 2.4-litre: size: 2483cc; cylinder: six; carb: twin solex (2.4/Mark 2) Twin SU (240); bore and stroke: 83mm x 76.5mm; BHP: 112@5750rpm (2.4) 120@5750 (Mark 2); 133@5500 (240).

3.4-litre; size: 3442cc; cylinders: six; carb: twin SU; bore and stroke: 83mm x 106mm; BHP: 210@5500rpm.

Mark 2s had more substantial seating than the earlier cars, now fitted with occasional tables.

The very last Mark 2s and the 240/340s didn't have the occasional tables.

The new dashboard layout for the Mark 2 that followed through to all subsequent Jaguar models up to the late 1960s.

An interesting comparison between the styling of the 2.4/3.4-litre (left) and Mark 2 models.

Similar comparisons between the black 3.4-litre and white 3.4-litre Mark 2.

3.8-litre; size: 3781cc; cylinders: six; carb: twin SU; bore and stroke: 87mm x 106mm; BHP: 220@5500.
Gearbox: four-speed manual, floor mounted gear change; ratios: 1st 15.35 (2.4), 11.95 (3.4/3.8), 14.42 (Mk2 2.4); 2nd 9.01 (2.4), 6.58 (3.4/3.8), 7.94 (Mk2 2.4); 3rd 6.22 (2.4), 4.54 (3.4/3.8), 5.48 (Mk2 2.4); 4th 4.55 (2.4), 3.54 (3.4/3.8), 4.27 (Mk2 2.4); three-speed automatic, dash and column mounted change; ratios: low 17.6 to 7.8; Intermediate 10.95 to 8.16; top 3.54.
Brakes: 2.4-litre (early): Lockheed Brakemaster hydraulic vacuum assisted drums all round.
2.4/3.4-litre (later) and Mark 2s: Dunlop hydraulic vacuum assisted discs all round.
Mark 2/240/340:
Rear axle: live axle.
Suspension: front: independent semi-trailing double wishbone, coil springs torsion and anti-roll bar; rear: parallel radius arms, Panhard rod, half-elliptic leaf springs.
Steering: Burman with power assistance, later option of power assistance.
Tyres: 6.40 x 15.

DIMENSIONS: length: 15ft 0.75in; **width:** 5ft 6.75in; **height:** 4ft. 9.5in; **wheelbase:** 8ft 11.375in; **track**: front 4ft 6.6in, rear 4ft 2.1in; **weight:** 27cwt (2.4), 28.5cwt (3.4/Mk2 2.4/3.4/240/340), 30cwt (3.8).

All Mark 1 and Mark 2 radiator grilles incorporated coloured badges to differentiate the engine size - 2.4-, 3.4- or 3.8 litre.

The rear end styling for the 240/340 models required a deep lower valance.

The 240/340 models with revised slimline bumper bars and removal of auxiliary lighting. Note the new style hubcaps.

The very last of the Mark 2s and some export models didn't have the flush-mounted auxiliary lighting; instead, it was replaced with mock horn grilles.

E-TYPE

The E-Type was Jaguar's successor to the XK sports cars – a car to some extent conceived from the D-Type's racing successes in the 1950s. An aerodynamically styled monocoque construction, the engine and front suspension were mounted on subframes, while at the rear a new independent suspension was encapsulated in a cage, complete with in-board disc brakes, driveshafts and differential. The engine was Jaguar's largest version of the XK unit at this time, 3781cc with triple SU carburettors, producing a phenomenal 265bhp and a maximum speed of 150mph. Just two body styles were initially available: a two-seater roadster with quick-action fold-down hood, and a fixed-head coupé with rear hatch to accommodate sufficient luggage to warrant Jaguar calling the new cars 'Grand Tourers', instead of out-and-out sports cars.

The aerodynamic body offered the ultimate in modern styling with its extensive one-piece bonnet, flush-mounted headlamps, a 'mouth' instead of a conventional radiator grille and a fast-back that made it look as though it was doing 100mph when standing still!

The early E-Type 3.8-litre fixed-head coupé shows the external chromed bonnet escutcheon, one per side, to open the bonnet. Later, these were replaced by internal locks.

The early E-Type 3.8-litre roadster, again showing the bonnet lock and the neatly fitting hood.

The iconic frontal view of an E-Type, in this case, a Series 1 with the enclosed headlights, triple windscreen wipers, and the interior rear-view mirror on an adjustable stem.

The purposeful yet practical fastback treatment for the E-Type Series 1 fixed-head coupé. All Series 1 models feature the twin closely positioned exhaust tailpipes.

The interior of the 3.8-litre E-Type with alloy panels, bucket seats, and the famous three-spoke wood-rim steering wheel.

Internally the E-Type featured the same dashboard layout as the Mark 2 saloon but without wood veneer. Instead, it had a mix of leather, Ambla and aluminium, with twin bucket seats, prominent centre console and a three-spoke wood-rimmed steering wheel that would become synonymous with the model.

In 1964, the E-Type received a number of improvements. The engine was enlarged to 4235cc capacity, mated to a four-speed all-synchromesh gearbox and an improved servo braking system. Internally the aluminium trim finishing was replaced by black fabric and new more comfortable seating was fitted. Apart from badging, there were no discernible differences to the exterior.

In 1966 an extra model joined the range, the 2+2, offering occasional rear seating. To achieve this the body structure was extended by 9in and the roof raised by 3in with a revised rake to the windscreen and new wider doors. Having a longer wheelbase enabled the fitting of automatic transmission, ideally suited to the US market.

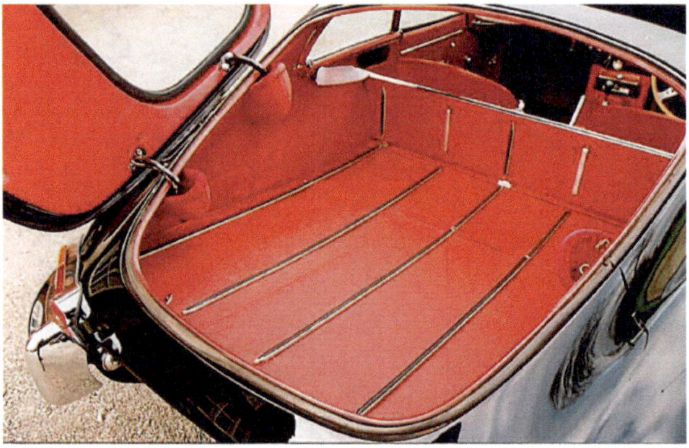

Superb luggage accommodation in the E-Type fixed-head coupé.

A later 4.2-litre E-Type roadster, visually identical to the 3.8-litre cars except for badging on the boot lid.

The revised interior for the 4.2-litre Series 1 models with black trim instead of alloy, and more comfortable seating.

4.2-litre Series 1 E-Types were differentiated from the 3.8-litre models by the boot badge.

Series 1 and 2 roadsters could be supplied with this factory glass-fibre hardtop, either finished in black or to the car's body colour.

The E-Type Series 1 2+2 model, note the extended doors, chrome trim below the window, and the raised roofline.

Some 1967 models were later known as Series 1½, with uncovered headlights and some interior trim changes, produced during the changeover to Series 2 models.

The following year, due to changes in Federal regulations in the States, the E-Type had to adopt revised lighting, leaving the headlights exposed, and in many cases the fitting of emissions equipment and different carburettors. This led to the introduction of the Series 2 models in 1968, available in all three body styles. Changes included a revised bonnet with a larger 'mouth' to improve airflow, further new lighting front and rear, a modified interior with a degree of crash-padding, flush-mounted door handles and semi-flush-fit rocker switches. For the first time, E-Types were available with steel wheels as well as wire versions.

In 1971, Jaguar released only its second new engine since the war: an excellent, well-engineered 12-cylinder V unit of 5.3 litres, fitted with four Stromberg carburettors, developing 272bhp. As with the original XK engine in 1948, the new V12 was fitted to a sporting model initially, in this case the E-Type, known as the Series 3. Initially promoted as also being available with the XK six-cylinder engine, only a handful were produced.

A significantly re-engineered monocoque was necessary, with widened wheelarches to accommodate larger wheels and brakes. The 'mouth' of the bonnet now incorporated a chromed grille. Using only the longer wheelbase of the previous 2+2, there were now only two body styles: a two-seater roadster and a 2+2 fixed-head coupé. Internally, it was more of what had gone before, but with a new smaller diameter leather trimmed steering wheel.

Although the model found some good early success, by 1973 the fixed-head had been deleted, while the roadster continued into 1974, albeit with some active promotion to keep sales motivated. The last 50 cars produced were known as Commemorative models, carrying a brass plaque on the dashboard signed by Sir William Lyons himself. Forty-nine of these cars were finished in black paintwork.

The Series 2 E-Type is identifiable from the front by the larger mouth, modified lighting, and bumper treatment. Series 2s were now also offered with steel wheels and hubcaps, as seen here.

The revised rear styling of the Series 2 with new lighting and backing panel, full-width bumper bar, and separated twin exhausts.

2+2 seating was available on the longer wheelbase fixed-heads for the Series 1, 2, and 3 models.

Total E-Type production amounted to some 72,500 examples, almost double that of the 1950s XKs, a model that has had a significant impact on Jaguar and the motoring world, even to this day.

NUMBERS PRODUCED: Series 1 3.8-litre roadster: 7818; Series 1 3.8-litre fixed-head coupé: 7663; Series 1 4.2-litre roadster: 9551; Series 1 4.2-litre fixed-head coupé: 7771; Series 1 4.2-litre 2+2: 5586; Series 2 4.2-litre roadster: 8641; Series 2 4.2-litre fixed-head coupé: 4878; Series 2 4.2-litre 2+2: 5529; Series 3 V12 roadster: 7982; Series 3 V12 2+2: 7310.
PRICES WHEN NEW: Series 1 3.8-litre roadster: £2098; Series 1 3.8-litre fixed-head coupé: £2197; Series 1 4.2-litre roadster: £1896; Series 1 4.2-litre fixed-head coupé: £1992; Series 1 4.2-litre 2+2: £2385; Series 2 4.2-litre roadster: £2163; Series 2 4.2-litre fixed-head coupé: £2273; Series 2 4.2-litre 2+2: £2512; Series 3 V12 roadster: £3139; Series 3 V12 2+2: £3383;
COLOURS: Series 1: Cream, Pearl Grey, Mist Grey, Cotswold Blue, Sherwood Green, Black, Carmen Red, Opalescent Gunmetal, Opalescent Silver Grey, Opalescent Silver Blue, Opalescent Blue, Opalescent Dark Green, Opalescent Maroon, Opalescent Golden Sand, Black, Claret, Imperial Maroon, Indigo Blue, British Racing Green, Sand, Primrose, Bronze, Warwick Grey, Beige, Willow Green; **Series 2**: Black, British Racing Green, Cream, Signal

Comparison view of Series 2s, showing the marked difference in glass and roofline between the two-seater fixed-head and the 2+2.

The Series 3 (V12) E-Type 2+2 is identifiable from the sides by the widened wheelarches and larger wheels/tyres.

The Series 3 roadster: still a two-seater, but produced only on the longer wheelbase monocoque.

Series 3 roadster with a factory-fitted hardtop. Note the changes to the rear-end styling again and the shaped exhaust tailpipes. Early examples were fitted with a four-outlet tailpipe.

Red, Warwick Grey, Ascot Fawn, Dark Blue, Light Blue, Primrose, Regency Red, Sable, Willow Green, Old English White; **Series 3**: Ascot Fawn, Black, British Racing Green, Dark Blue, Light Blue, Primrose, Sable, Signal Red, Warwick Grey, Willow Green, Old English White Sable, Azure Blue, Fern Grey, Greensand, Heather, Lavender Blue, Regency Red, Silver Grey, Turquoise.

TECHNICAL: Engines: 3.8-litre: size: 3781cc; cylinders: six; carb: Triple SU; bore & stroke: 87mm x 106mm; BHP: 265@5500.
4.2-litre: size: 4235cc; cylinders: six; carb: Triple SU (US Twin Stromberg); bore & stroke: 92.07mm x 106mm; BHP: 265bhp@5400rpm.

The interior of the Series 3 models, very similar to Series 2 with the toggle switches on the dashboard, flush door handles. The seats now have head restraints, and the steering wheel has changed to leather-covered.

5.3-litre: size: 5353cc; cylinders: 12; carb: Quad Stromberg; bore & stroke: 90mm x 70mm; BHP: 272@5850rpm.
Gearbox: four-speed manual, floor mounted gear change; ratios: 1st 11.18 (3.8), 8.23 (4.2), 9.0 (5.3) ; 2nd 6.16 (3.8), 5.34 (4.2), 5.86 (5.3); 3rd 4.25 (3.8), 3.90 (4.2), 4.27 (5.3); 4th 3.31 3.07 (4.2/5.3); alternative ratios: 4.09, 3.77, 3.07, 3.27; three-speed automatic, floor mounted change; ratios: low

The striking view of the Series 3 front, now featuring a proper grille.

Headlight surround treatment varied throughout production, from this Series 1 ...

... to the interim Series 1½ ...

... to Series 2 ...

... and finally Series 3.

A quick-reference frontal view of the E-Type through the years. In the centre is the Series 1, flanked on the right by the Series 2 and on the left by the Series 3.

6.91; intermediate 4.20; top 2.88.
Brakes: Series 1 and 2: Dunlop discs all round, vacuum assisted; Series 3: Girling discs all round (vented at front), vacuum assisted.
Suspension: front: independent wishbone, torsion bars, anti-roll bar ; rear: independent lower wishbone, upper driveshaft link, radius arms, coil springs, anti-roll bar.
Steering: rack and pinion.
Tyres: Series 1 and 2: 6.40 x 15; Series 3: E70VR – 15.

DIMENSIONS: length: 14ft 7.5in (std), 15ft 4.5in (2+2/Ser 3); **width:** 5ft 4.25in; **height:** 3ft 11in (Ser 1 & 2 rster), 4ft (Ser 1 & 2 fhc), 4ft 2.5in (2+2); **wheelbase:** 8ft (Ser 1 & 2), 8ft 9in (Ser 1 & 2 2+2); **track**: front: 4ft 2in (std), 4ft 6.5in (Ser 3); rear: 4ft 2in (std), 4ft 5in (Ser 3); **weight:** 24cwt (Ser 1 & 2 rster), 24.1cwt (Ser 1 fhc), 25.1cwt (Ser 1 & 2 4.2 fhc), 27.5cwt (2+2), 28.8cwt (Ser 3 rster), 29.5cwt (Ser 3 2+2).

MARK X/420G

Jaguar's 'flagship' saloons of the 1950s (Mark VII to IX), although highly successful, were looking old by the end of the decade, and along with Jaguar's technological advancements and changing market trends, a new car was needed, that being the Mark X released in October 1961.

An entirely new monocoque bodyshell was a unique style for the model, the largest Jaguar had ever produced and one that carried the dubious accolade of being the widest British production car at the time. It was longer than its predecessors, wider but much lower, giving the car a low-slung look. The car was massive by any standards, with more room under the bonnet than any previous Jaguar, an incredibly large boot area, and rear compartment legroom to match most limousines.

The Mark X incorporated the E-Type's triple carburettor XK engine with manual or

The Mark X had a rather bulbous body without side adornment. It was the first Jaguar to feature a broader radiator grille that leaned forward, with a new small-sized leaper mascot on the bonnet. Additionally, it was the first Jaguar to feature four headlights. The bonnet was hinged at the front.

The only frontal difference between the Mark X and 420G was the centre rib in the radiator grille.

Rear view of a 420G (the same as the Mark X), except for the badging on the boot lid.

Interior of a 3.8-litre Mark X with the simplistic three-button heater controls on the centre console below the radio.

automatic transmission, along with the same car's independent rear suspension package and disc brakes all round.

Inside, there were acres of space with occupants cocooned in extra-wide seating (reclining at the front), sitting low at sill level within the very wide floorpan, emphasised by the outward slopping doors. The dashboard followed that of the Mark 2 and all subsequent 1960s models, but with extra curvature at the corners, a different wood veneer and even a vacuum-controlled heating system with separate outlets for the rear seat passengers. A touch of Jaguar traditionalism included front seatback-mounted veneered occasional tables.

The rear low-set seating accommodation provided more than adequate headroom, with the usual traditional features like the veneered occasional tables.

The 4.2-litre Mark X had a modified heating/ventilation system with separate controls for each side of the car, seen here below the centre dashboard panel.

Following the same changes as the E-Type in 1964, the Mark X received the larger 4.2-litre engine, all-synchromesh gearbox (as well as a new automatic transmission), a new Varamatic power assisted steering and a revised heating/ventilation system.

A limousine model could be specified to special order. The only difference to the standard saloon was the fitting of a fixed front seating arrangement with a glass division separating the driver/front seat passenger from the rear compartment. This incorporated a magazine rack in the centre between the occasional tables.

The next change came in 1967 when Jaguar re-designated the Mark X as the 420G. The only other changes were cosmetic, with different hub caps, a vertical prominent rib to the radiator grille, the option of duotone exterior paint finishes with a painted coachline or, for single colour paints, a chromed swage line trim from front to rear of the car, in both cases with front wing repeater indicators.

Inside, the 420G dashboard now had padded area to the top rail along with the inclusion of the clock in the centre (replacing that fitted in the rev counter before). A different type of carpet and ventilated leather panels were featured in the seats.

The 420G stayed in limited production until 1970 after the introduction of its replacement, the XJ6, in 1968, with some cars not registered until 1971.

Many aspects of the Mark X/420G lived on. In 1968, by which time Jaguar was part of the British Leyland Group, a new Daimler was also released, the DS420 limousine. It was

One of the rare limousine models produced with a centre division.

A 420G model with Jaguar's new style hub caps fitted to all cars post 1967. The addition of the chromed swage line trim and front wing indicator repeaters are the only side view differences to the Mark Xs.

Where a duotone paint scheme was ordered, the chromed swage line trim was deleted in favour of a coachline.

Interior of a 420G with the black padded areas, the dash-top mounted clock, and perforated leather upholstery. This is a rare manual transmission model, as most Mark X/420Gs were supplied with automatic transmission.

The Mark X/420G was the first Jaguar to be available with the factory-fitted option of electric windows, operated from this panel on the centre console between the front seats.

to be a replacement for the ageing traditional Daimler Majestic Major and the also aged Vanden Plas Princess from the old BMC range.

The styling of the new Daimler owed much to Sir William Lyons, and the car took a lot from the Jaguar Mark X/420G parts bin, including the floorpan, inner wing sections, some trim and a detuned version of the 4.2-litre XK engine. Even the front end styling resembled the Mark X, with some 'Daimlerisation'.

NUMBERS PRODUCED: Mark X 3.8-litre: 12,961; Mark X 4.2-litre: 5672; 420G: 5542.
PRICES WHEN NEW: Mark X 3.8-litre: £2392; Mark X 4.2-litre: £2167; 420G: £2237.
COLOURS: Mark X: Cream, Pearl Grey, Mist Grey, Cotswold Blue, Sherwood Green, Black, Carmen Red, Opalescent Silver Grey, Opalescent Gunmetal, Opalescent Silver Blue, Opalescent Blue, Opalescent Bronze, Opalescent Golden Sand, Opalescent Dark Green, Opalescent Maroon, Warwick Grey, Dark Blue, Primrose; **420G**: Cream, Warwick Grey, Ascot Fawn, Sable, Regency Red, Willow Green, British Racing Green, Light Blue, Dark Blue, Black. Duotones: Black over Ascot Fawn, Black over Warwick Grey, Dark Blue over Light Blue, British Racing Green over Willow Green, Black over Golden Sand, Black over Opalescent Silver Grey, Dark Blue over Opalescent Silver Blue.
TECHNICAL: **Engines:** 3.8-litre: size: 3781cc; cylinders: six; carb: triple SU; bore & stroke: 87mm x 106mm; BHP: 265@55004.
2-litre: size: 4235cc; cylinders: six; carb: triple SU; bore & stroke: 92.07mm x 106mm; BHP: 265bhp@5400rpm.
Gearbox: four-speed manual, floor mounted gear change; ratios: 1st 11.95 (3.8) 10.76 (4.2), 2nd 6.54 (3.8) 6.98 (4.2), 3rd 4.54 (3.8) 4.70 (4.2); 4th 3.54 (3.8/4.2); three-speed automatic, column mounted change; ratios: low 17 to 6 to 8.16 (3.8) to 8.5 (4.2); intermediate 10.95 to 5.08 (3.8) to 5.16 (4.2); top 3.54.
Brakes: Dunlop discs all round, with vacuum assisted.
Suspension: front Independent semi trailing double wishbone, coil springs, anti-roll bar; rear independent lower wishbone, upper driveshaft link, radius arms, coil springs.
Steering: Burman recirculating ball.
Tyres: 7.50 x 14.
DIMENSIONS: length: 16ft 10in; **width:** 6ft 4in; **height:** 4ft 6.75in; **wheelbase:** 10ft; **track**: front 4ft 10in, rear 4ft 10in; **weight:** 37cwt.

'S'/420

The early sixties saw tremendous sales success for Jaguar with its completely new model range. Yet there was an opportunity to further expand its market share with the addition of another new model, using as many components from the parts bins as possible to keep costs down and enhance profits.

For a brief period from 1963 to 1968, the 'S' was available (now commonly known as the S-Type, although confused with a much more modern model – see later). It was a mix-and-match using the centre section of the Mark 2 (but a modified roof area), and a revised frontal aspect with new front wings, different lighting and radiator grille. At the rear, the floorpan was completely redesigned to accommodate the independent suspension from the Mark X/E-Type, also allowing for a larger boot area, new wings and rear end styling, a somewhat smaller version of the Mark X. Internally, again a mix of a slightly revised dashboard arrangement, new centre console, revised seating, new door panels and marginally more legroom for rear seat passengers.

Mechanically, apart from the rear suspension, the 'S' was as the Mark 2. However, being priced a step above the former,

The 'S' incorporated a raised roof area with a larger rear window and Mark X-styled rear end. The twin exhaust pipes are also now separated, previously together on the sister Mark 2 range.

The 1960s 'S' model with a revised front end. Slimline bumpers set the pattern for the later Mark 2 (240/340) models. New front wings incorporated peaks over the headlights and inset auxiliary lights, and Mark X-style indicator/side light units were fitted. The radiator grille is unique to this model.

The interior of the 'S', although utilising the same dashboard as the Mark 2, featured a new under-dash parcel shelf, centre console, and heater controls. The door trims and seats were also new to this model.

The last of the Mark 2s (240) alongside the 'S'.

the 'S' was only fitted with the two larger six-cylinder engines.

Yet another (extra) mid-sized saloon entered the range in 1966: the 420. This came about as Jaguar were still working on an entirely new saloon (XJ6) but with concerns about the popularity of the Mark X/420G and the Mark 2 seven years old, it was felt that an interim model was needed.

Basically, the 420 was an 'S' with three major differences. Fitted with a larger 4.2-litre version of the XK engine in twin-carburettor form, it also benefited from a more efficient cooling system and had power assisted steering as standard.

Externally, from the scuttle back it was pure 'S', but the front was very much a scaled-down version of the Mark X with a new squatter grille, four headlights and new wings and bonnet.

It was also the first Daimler model (called the 420 Sovereign) to be purely badge-engineered from the Jaguar, with revised badging and fluted radiator grille.

Internally, the 420 had another revised dashboard arrangement with the same layout and instrumentation, but the top rail was padded black with a clock in the centre and revised wood panelling to the end panels. Marginally changes took place in areas like the door trims and other woodwork, otherwise it was as the 'S'.

Sold at a premium price over the 'S', it was only available with the 4.2-litre engine with manual/overdrive or automatic transmission.

In 1967, Jaguar began to refine its saloon range, slowly leading to the demise of all the existing cars after the introduction of its

The 'S' was a very well-balanced design offering advantages of ride, comfort, and space over the Mark 2. Although many cars (like this one) were fitted with wire wheels, the standard fit was still steel wheels to body colour plus chromed hub caps.

Comparison between the Mark 2 and 'S' showing the raised roofline for interior comfort, larger rear window, and extended boot space.

new XJ6 in 1968. This process started with the changes to the Mark 2 range in 1967 as discussed in an earlier chapter.

By 1968 it was the turn of the 'S' model to be dropped from the range, with the 3.8-litre leaving production in June, while the 3.4-litre soldiered on until August.

The 420s faired slightly better, the Jaguar ending production in September 1968, while the Daimler 420 Sovereign continued until 1969.

The 'S' grille, although looking very similar to the Mark 2, had a more pronounced surround.

NUMBERS PRODUCED: 3.4-litre 'S': 9928; 3.8-litre 'S': 15,075; 420: 10,236 (16,060 with Daimler 420 Sovereign).
PRICES WHEN NEW: 3.4-litre 'S': £1669; 3.8-litre 'S': £1758; 420: £1930.
COLOURS: 'S': Cream, Beige, Warwick Grey, British Racing Green, Dark Blue, Black, Carmen Red, Opalescent Silver Grey, Opalescent Silver Blue, Opalescent Golden Sand, Opalescent Dark Green, Opalescent Maroon; **420**: Cream, Beige, Warwick Grey, Willow Green, British Racing Green, Dark Blue, Black, Opalescent Golden Sand, Opalescent Silver Grey, Opalescent Silver Blue, Opalescent Maroon.
TECHNICAL: **Engines:** 3.4-litre: size: 3442cc; cylinders: six; carb: twin SU; bore & stroke: 83mm x 106mm; BHP: 210@5500rpm.
3.8-litre: size: 3781cc; cylinders: six; carb: twin SU; bore & stroke: 87mm x 106mm; BHP: 220@5500.
4.2-litre: size: 4235cc; cylinders: six; car: twin SU; bore & stroke: 92.07 x 106mm; BHP: 245@5500rpm.
Gearbox: four-speed manual, floor-mounted gear change; ratios: 1st 11.95 (3.4/3.8), 10.76 (4.2); 2nd 6.58 (3.4/3.8), 6.97 (4.2); 3rd 4.54 (3.4/3.8), 4.70 (4.2); 4th 3.54; three-speed automatic, column mounted change; ratios: low 17.6 to 7.8 (3.4/3.8), 4.48 to 2.40 (4.2); intermediate 10.95 to 8.16 (3.4/3.8), 2.92 to 1.46 (4.2); top 3.54.
Brakes: 'S': Dunlop discs all round, vacuum assisted; 420: Girling discs all round, vacuum-assisted.

The 420 showing the revised front treatment. The mock rectangular horn grilles were unique to this model.

Comparison front-end view of the 'S' and 420.

Dashboard revisions for the 420 from the 'S' included new shaped veneered panels and upper dash padded area with an integrated clock.

Suspension: front independent semi-trailing double wishbone, coil springs, torsion and anti-roll bar; rear independent, lower wishbone/ upper driveshaft link, radius arms, twin coil springs.
Steering: Burman with power assistance, later option of power assistance.
Tyres: 6.40 x 5.
DIMENSIONS: length: 15ft 7in ('S') 15ft 7.5in (420); **width:** 5ft 6.25in ('S') 5ft 7in (420); **height:** 4ft 7.75in ('S') 4ft 8.25in (420); **wheelbase:** 8ft 11.5in; **track**: front 4ft 7.25in ('S'), 4ft 7.5in (420); rear: 4ft 6.25in; **weight:** 32cwt (3.4), 33cwt (3.8/4.2).

XJ SERIES 1, 2 & 3

In September 1968, Jaguar announced its single successor to all the 1960s saloons, the XJ6. Although embracing much of the previous models' mechanical aspects, a revised front suspension with new tyre technology ensured the new car was more refined and handled better. Retaining the XK engine from the outgoing 420, with its twin SU carburettors, a smaller 2.8-litre variant was also offered, ideally suited to markets that were tax sensitive. Both engines came with the all-synchromesh four-speed gearbox with overdrive, or as a three-speed automatic transmission.

The rather squared-off look of the XJ Series 1 with engine size identified by badging. Early cars didn't feature a 'Jaguar' badge on the boot (where the GB plate is fitted on this car), and the straight exhaust tailpipes are a sign of an early car.

Stylistically it was all new, although still very much of the Jaguar character, with the four-headlight treatment but no auxiliary lights, and with an 'egg-crate' chromed grille and no leaper mascot on the bonnet. The side elevation included a Coke-bottle 'lift' over the rear wings and a squared-off boot area. Devoid of most badging, the design was still instantly recognisable as a Jaguar.

The interior was also new, with a modified approach to the instruments and switch-gear, though retaining the same layout so well known from the Mark 2 and beyond. A new centre console, seating and door trims plus a new heating/ventilation system with adjustable face outlets, were accompanied by the continued use of wood veneer in the best Jaguar tradition.

Initially it was offered purely as a Jaguar, but the following year was available as a Daimler Sovereign, and later longer-wheelbase

The original XJ6 Series 1. The Webasto sunroof was not a standard factory feature. This car is fitted with chromed steel wheel rims, an optional extra.

Later Series 1 with the 'Jaguar' badge and the 'kinked' exhaust tailpipes, done apparently due to exhaust gases being forced back inside the car when windows were open.

Interior of the XJ6 Series 1 with a similar instrument layout to earlier cars but with new legends and switchgear. Note the use of alloy finishing panels for the centre console. Later Series 1 models had matt black instrument surrounds instead of the chrome shown here.

Comparisons of the short and long-wheelbase models, with the extra length in the rear doors.

models were offered. The Daimlers were essentially badge-engineered Jaguars by this time.

The XJ's bodyshell was always designed to take the V12 engine, initially launched in the 1971 E-Type. This became available in 1972 as the Jaguar XJ12 or Daimler Double Six, followed by an even more upmarket Daimler variant, the Double Six Vanden Plas. The most expensive of all the XJs, the Vanden Plas, partly assembled in Coventry, was taken down to the Vanden Plas Coachworks in London where it was painted in a bespoke range

XJ12 Series 1 had a more conventional radiator grille. The auxiliary lighting was an option.

The XJ6 Series 1 in its original standard form with steel wheels painted silver, with hub caps and rimbellishers.

of colours, with an Everflex roof covering, upholstered in all-leather different styled seating, with better quality wood veneer with boxwood inlays.

For the 1974 model year, the original XJ6/XJ12 cars became known as the Series 1, with the announcement of the Series 2 models. Not obviously different to the earlier cars, the Series 2 cars had actually changed considerably.

Stylistically, the front showed the most significant exterior changes. To meet regulation requirements in the USA, the bumper level was raised necessitating a new shallower radiator

A Series 2 model, the only visual differences from the side view are the raised front bumper height and the change to a preformed steel wheel.

US regulations demanded a revised bumper level, so the Series 2 had a new style, leaving space beneath for a different valance and trim including the side/indicator light units and, of course, a new shallower radiator grille.

grille, revised lighting and a new valance. New lighting and trim also applied to the rear; otherwise, the centre body area remained as the earlier cars, initially in both short and long-wheelbase versions. These were the first Jaguars to feature impact safety bars within the doors.

Internally, the Series 2 had an entirely new dashboard layout, instruments and switchgear, as well as revised trim in other areas. They were the first cars to feature fibre-optic lighting for some of the switchgear, and, with a revised bulkhead arrangement, many connections passed through from the engine compartment

The Series 2 rear, the most notable change being the movement of the number plate illumination to the boot lid with an integrated boot lock.

The most attractive of all the XJs is the two-door coupé, with its pillarless construction, and all of this model were fitted with the vinyl roof. The Kent alloy wheels became an optional fit until the end of Series 3 production.

Series 2 interior with a complete change of layout and switchgear.

via multi-pin connectors, rather than through holes and grommets. A new comprehensive air-conditioning system was adopted, and there were new types of upholstery options.

Mechanically, the 2.8-litre engine finally gave way to a new 3.4-litre version, while the 4.2-litre and V12 units were still available for both Daimler and Jaguar, in either wheelbase, although later the short-wheelbase versions were dropped. The upmarket Daimler Double Six Vanden Plas model was continued in Series 2 form, now joined by a 4.2-litre version.

To accompany the other Series 2 models was an entirely new, very attractive two-door fixed-head coupé on the shorter wheelbase. Jaguar and Daimler 4.2 and 5.3-litre models were available with a vinyl roof covering, and, due to the pillarless construction, the side

Leather seating was the norm, and even the coupé had comfortable rear seating …

… a choice of other trim materials became available with the Series 2 model.

Major styling changes came with the Series 3. A larger glass area, raised roof line, flush-mounted door handles, rubber-faced bumper bars, another new radiator grille and lighting, and a complex design of spring-fitted hub caps for the steel-wheeled cars.

glasses could be wound down totally out of sight, making for a very attractive open coupé format.

The Series 2 models were even more successful than the Series 1 cars, despite this being in the middle of British Leyland's bad era with unsettled industrial relations, poor parts supply and bad build quality. All the Series 2 cars left production in 1978 when the revised Series 3 models were announced.

For the first time in the company's history, Jaguar approached an outside styling house to renew the Series XJ: Pininfarina in Italy. Its brief was to modernise the car, given Jaguar was not in a position to launch an entirely new saloon at the time. The result was a car that looked like the previous XJs, but was 'sharper' in style with up to-date features.

Every body panel came in for revision yet retained the overall style of the original. There was a larger glass area and a flatter roof, another new radiator grille, lights and flush-mounted door handles plus energy-absorbing rubber faced bumper bars.

Internally, although the basic design remained unchanged from the Series 2, there were many, sometimes subtle, changes as well as new seating, door trims and much more. Mechanically, it was much the same, except that fuel-injection was now the norm for most engines.

The range of models was much as

before, but as the years went by, names and specifications changed. As far as the UK was concerned, the Series 3s lost the Vanden Plas name in 1982, and in 1983 a new top-of-the-range Jaguar XJ was released, called the Sovereign (stealing a name previously used for Daimler models). Trim and equipment levels were consistently upgraded, and even a 'fleet' 3.4-litre model was produced with less trim, to try to capture a new market.

Rear-end styling for the Series 3s was tidied up, all new, including the much larger rear screen.

A post-1993 XJ Series 3 with the later Pepperpot alloy wheels, a common fitment, standard on the upmarket Sovereign model.

A useful comparison between the Series 2 and Series 3 models.

Comparison of rear-end styling treatment between the Series 2 and Series 3 models.

The earlier Series 3 interior, in some respects very similar to the Series 2 …

… the early style of centre console and controls …

… and the later type, in this case fitted with Jaguar's first on-board computer.

A range of different trims were offered according to model. In this case the base 'fleet' Series 3 with fabric upholstery (also available with cloth), also having straight grain wood veneer. Note the later centre console, fitted with the clock (upmarket models get the on-board computer as in the previous picture).

XJ12 comparisons, Series 1 and late Series 3.

The Series 3 lasted well beyond its years, a testament to its success. The last six-cylinder model left production in April 1987, the last Jaguar V12 in November 1991, and the last Daimler in November 1992. From a body styling perspective, it was Jaguar's most successful car ever, and design elements have continued to come through in later styling.

NUMBERS PRODUCED: XJ6 Series 1 2.8-litre: 19,322 (22,555 including Daimlers); XJ6 Series 1 4.2-litre: 59,951 (71,859 including Daimlers); XJ12 Series 1: 3228 (4113 including Daimlers); XJ6 Series 2 2.8-litre: 170; XJ6 Series 2 3.4-litre: 6880 (9221 including Daimlers); XJ6 Series 2 4.2-litre: 69,951 (87,800 including Daimlers); XJ12 Series 2: 16,010 (20,344 including Daimlers); XJ6 coupé: 6487 (8164 including Daimlers); XJ12 coupé: 1855 (2262 including Daimlers); XJ6 Series 3 3.4-litre: 5799; XJ6 Series 3 4.2-litre: 113,695 (127,164 including Daimlers); XJ12 Series 3: 12,643 (54,542 including Daimlers).

PRICES WHEN NEW: XJ6 Series 1 2.8-litre: £1797; XJ6 Series 1 4.2-litre: £2254; XJ12 Series 1: £2474; XJ6 Series 2 3.4-litre: £6880; XJ6 Series 2 4.2-litre: £3674; XJ12 Series 2: £4702; XJ6 coupé: £4260; XJ12 coupé: £5181; XJ6 Series 3 3.4-litre: £11,189; XJ6 Series 3 4.2-litre: £12,326; XJ12 Series 3: £15,014.

COLOURS: Series 1: Old English White, Warwick Grey, Ascot Fawn, Willow Green, Dark Blue, Sable, Light Blue, British Racing Green, Regency Red, Black, Signal Red, Primrose, Azure Blue, Light Silver, Fern Grey, Turquoise, Greensand, Heather, Lavender; plus specials for Vanden Plas models: Silver Sand, Caramel, Coral, Aegean Blue, Sage Green, Morello Cherry, Aubergine; **Series 2**: All the above plus: Juniper Green, Carriage Brown, Moroccan Bronze, Squadron Blue; **Series 3**: Tudor White, Cotswold Yellow, Damson Red, Racing Green Metallic, Racing Green, Silver Frost, Cobalt Blue, Quartz Blue, Chestnut Brown, Sebring Red, Black, Indigo Blue, Grosvenor Brown, Portland Beige, Rhodium Silver, Sapphire Blue, Coronet Gold, Sable, Claret, Silversand, Clarendon Blue, Cirrus Grey, Cranberry, Antelope, Sage Green, Regent Grey, Windsor Grey, Steel Blue, Curlew Brown, Nimbus White, Grenadier Red, Alpine Green, Arctic Blue, Bordeaux, Crimson, Dorchester Grey, Moorland Green, Satin Beige, Silver Birch, Solent Blue, Sovereign Gold, Talisman Silver, Tungsten Grey, Glacier White, Westminster Blue, Savoy Grey, Jade Green, Gunmetal, Regency Red, Brooklands Green, Diamond Blue, Oyster, Tuscany Bronze; plus specials for Vanden Plas models: Silversand, Caramel, Coral, Biascan Blue, Mistletoe, Mink, Amethyst.

TECHNICAL: Engines: 2.8-litre: size: 2791cc; cylinders: six; carb: twin SU; bore & stroke: 83mm x 86mm; BHP: 180@6000rpm.
3.4-litre: size: 3442cc; cylinders: six; carb: twin SU; bore & stroke: 83mm x 106mm; BHP: 161@5500rpm.
4.2-litre: size: 4235cc; cylinders: six; carb: twin SU (later fuel-injection); bore & stroke: 92.07 x 106mm; BHP: 245@5500rpm.
5.3-litre (V12): size: 5343cc; cylinders: 12; carb: quad Stromberg (later fuel-injection); bore & stroke: 90mm x 70mm; BHP: 253@6000rpm.

Gearbox: four-speed manual, floor mounted gear change; ratios: 1st 12.05 (2.8), 11.45 (3.4), 10.38 (4.2); 2nd 8.14 (2.8), 6.75 (3.4), 6.74 (4.2); 3rd 5.93 (2.8), 4.91 (3.4), 4.92 (4.2); 4th 4.27 (2.8), 3.54 (3.4/4.2); three-speed automatic, column mounted change; ratios: low 10.2 to 20.4 (2.8), 4.80 to 2.40 (3.4), 4.78 to 2.89 (4.2); 5.95 to 2.48 (5.3); intermediate 6.19 to 12.38 (2.8), 2.90 to 1.45 (3.4/4.2), 3.55 to 1.48 (5.3); top 4.27 (2.8), 3.54 (3.4/4.2), 3.07 (5.3).

Brakes: Girling, discs all round. Lockheed servo.

Suspension: front independent semi-trailing double wishbone, coil springs, anti-roll bar; rear independent, lower wishbone/upper driveshaft link, radius arms, twin coil springs.

Steering: rack and pinion with power assistance.

Tyres: E70 VR 15.

DIMENSIONS: length: 15ft 9.5in (swb), 16ft 2.75in) lwb); **width:** 5ft 9.25in; **height:** 4ft 6in; **wheelbase:** 9ft 0.75in (swb), 9ft 4.75in (lwb); **Track**: front 4ft 10in, rear 4ft 10.5in; **weight:** 33cwt (XJ6 swb), 34cwt (XJ6 lwb), 35cwt (XJ12 swb), 36cwt (XJ12 lwb).

XJ-S

After Jaguar's success with postwar sports cars, the XKs and E-Types, it, like many other manufacturers, considered the rakish two-seater sports car would not survive, particularly in valuable export markets like the USA where safety regulations were ever-tightening and customers' expectations were growing. The next new model would therefore be a true grand tourer rather than sports car, and in September 1975, the XJ-S was launched.

The basic architecture of the model was the short-wheelbase floorpan of the XJ saloon. The V12 engine and allied suspension/braking system was fitted and the pièce de resistance was the bodyshell designed by aerodynamicist Malcolm Sayer. A two-door 2+2 design that bore no resemblance to anything Jaguar or other manufacturers had produced before, the most striking aspect of it were the integrated 'wings' from the top rear of the roof down to the rear wings, that became known as 'flying buttresses'. Looking very modern, they were

The original XJ-S fitted with the standard-fit Kent alloy wheels, no side coachlines, shallow bonnet, and full rubber bumpers.

The XJ-S Pre-HE with the famous 'flying buttresses' coming down from the roof to the rear wings. This later 1970s model has a body-painted boot …

... whereas this earlier model has a matt black-painted panel on the boot.

not just cosmetic, actually aiding stability at speed, and the whole design was particularly aerodynamic for a production car of its day.

Another different aspect was the removal of features for which Jaguar became synonymous, like a conventional radiator grille, external chrome trim, and, internally, the lack of wood veneer, instead replaced by black vinyl and aluminium. A unique feature of the XJ-S was the use of bar gauges for the auxiliary instrumentation. This was a very 'new' car.

Initially fitted with only the 5.3-litre V12 engine with the option of automatic transmission or four-speed all-synchromesh gearbox, the latter proved unpopular and was dropped after just over 300 were sold. The V12 engine was fuel injected and offered performance up to the standard of the old E-Type Series 3, but in greater refinement, comfort and ride, due to its XJ heritage.

Jaguar marketed the XJ-S as a prime competitor to the likes of Mercedes and others, at a very attractive price, although in Jaguar terms it was the most expensive production car it had produced up to that time.

With concerns over build quality (still in the British Leyland era), poor fuel consumption, and not least the fact that the design was so

The interior of the earlier cars was well fitted out, with many trim items taken from the contemporary XJ saloons. Note the matt black finishes and lack of wood veneer. This is one of the rare four-speed manual transmission models.

The unique-to-the-model bar gauges and other instrument layout to the pre-face-lift XJ-S.

Full frontal view of the early XJ-S with the very shallow 'hump' in the bonnet.

new and 'unJaguarish', sales were not initially good. To motivate sales in the US, Jaguar teamed up with Group 44 to set up fairly successful racing exploits – for a while.

Jaguar's board almost dropped the car, but the new man at the helm, Sir John Egan, saw the benefits of the model, and it was revamped. In 1981, the HE (high efficiency) model replaced the original car with redesigned cylinder heads, creating what was called the 'fireball' head, so the XJ-S could now achieve up to 20mpg. Build quality was addressed and a few traditional Jaguar touches were reinstated. Elm wood veneer was added to the interior. To enhance the exterior, chrome blades were added to the new-style rubber bumpers, a swage coachline featured along the sides of the body, all of which improved the look, and, most importantly, the fortunes of the car.

The post-1981 HE model with Starfish alloy wheels and the twin coachline.

The post-1981 HE with a modicum of wood veneer (burr elm) and a lack of bright alloy trim.

Jaguar again got involved in competition in the early 1980s, with TWR (Tom Walkinshaw Racing). Competing with specially prepared XJ-Ss, it successfully raced in the European Touring Car Championship, winning outright in 1984, all of which improved the fortunes and sales further for the model.

HE and later V12 models with the growler badge on the bonnet and revised bumper bar treatment.

The post-HE sports a 'V12' badge on the boot lid, plus a revised bumper incorporating fog lamps.

One of the limited run of specially finished TWR (Tom Walkinshaw Racing) XJ-Ss; not the same as the factory-sponsored JaguarSport, later joint ventures.

In 1983, Jaguar introduced additional XJ-S models, the cabriolets and another engine, the AJ6 multi-valve six-cylinder unit. The cabriolet was a half-way house, as there was still demand for a soft top model, but Jaguar hadn't yet developed a conventional convertible.

The cabriolet was designed and built with the help of the Tickford company (part of Aston Martin), and involved standard coupés with the roof and buttresses cut off, assembled on the Browns Lane production line, but then shipped over to Tickford for final build and finishing. There, the trim was fitted: a manually operated rear hood and targa panels above the driver and passenger seats. The cabriolets were strictly a two-seater model, with the rear area fitted with a trimmed storage box and shelf. As the main aspects of interior trim were the same as the coupés, some owners chose later to fit coupé rear seating.

The new 3.6-litre engine (AJ6) was fitted

The XJ-S cabriolet model from the mid-1980s with the half hood and hard targa panels, shown here with the top up and down. Buyers had the option of the Starfish or Lattice alloy wheels.

A cabriolet with the top down. Note the support bar across the roof area which, because of apparent safety regulations, prevented the factory from fitting rear seats. Here, with the lidded box area, a similar version of which was also incorporated in the original convertible model.

The Jaguar XJ-S convertible as released in 1987 with a fully lined, electrically driven hood incorporating a heated glass rear screen.

to all XJ-S models, opening up a new market at a different price level. It was mated to either a three-speed automatic transmission or a new five-speed Getrag manual gearbox. A new bonnet panel was needed for the six-cylinder cars with a defined raised centre section, as the new engine needed extra height. This type of bonnet was later adopted for all XJS models.

The cabriolet didn't prove as popular as Jaguar had hoped in the USA, so an American coachbuilder, Hess & Eisenhardt, produced its own under license, built in small numbers for the domestic market. Jaguar learnt a lot from this exercise, and in 1987 launched its own production convertible for world markets to replace the cabriolets. Strictly a two-seater, built initially only on the V12 chassis with upmarket trim, it had a fully electrically operated lined hood, and was the first convertible to feature a heated glass rear screen instead of the usual Perspex type.

A joint venture was set up with TWR (the racing team that ran the XJ-Ss in the ETC), which later went on to campaign other Jaguar-engined cars, including a successful return to the renowned Le Mans 24-hour.

That new venture was called JaguarSport, and the XJ-S was a suitable vehicle for it to

The lavish interior of Jaguar's top-of-the-range convertible from 1988.

The JaguarSport 6.0-litre XJR-S.

modify, both in trim and performance levels with a range of specifications customers could request to special order. Called the XJR-S, they were available only through selected Jaguar dealers and continued in low-level production until 1993.

In 1991 major changes took place with the XJ-S, not least a revised name, now simply XJS (without the hyphen). As the car had been in production since 1975 the tooling was getting old, so Jaguar took the opportunity to carry out some redesigning.

Bodies were now made from galvanised metal offering better protection against

The special rear spoiler and bumper treatment for the XJR-S. Note the quad exhaust system.

There were numerous special edition XJ-S for various markets, in this case, the Collection Classic for the USA.

Comparison views of Jaguar's face-lifted XJS from 1991 alongside the earlier model.

Jaguar's new face-lifted XJS model from 1991 with smoothed-out lines.,

corrosion. Jaguar spent £50m on the project which included new panelling, although in most cases grafted over the existing superstructure. The overall lines were smoothed out with a new roof, raked windscreen, new rear wings with rounded corners, emulating to some extent the now 'corporate' look adopted with the new XJ saloon (see later section). Door windows were now frameless, door handles were flush-mounted and trim was altered.

Apart from some upholstery changes, the interior had a new dashboard layout with conventional analogue instrumentation instead of the old bar gauges of the previous models.

The V12 engine continued but the six-cylinder AJ6 engine was increased to 4.0 litres capacity with a revised gearbox. The 4.0-litre engine was also now made available as an additional convertible model. All these changes gave the XJS a new lease of life.

The next change came in 1993 with more engine developments. The 5.3-litre V12 gave way to a new 6.0-litre version and the AJ6 engine now gave way to the AJ16 unit, which incorporated individual coils over plugs ignition. Various trim changes took place, including the fitting of 2+2 seating in the convertibles.

Other changes followed throughout the rest of the XJS' life, mostly affecting interior and exterior trim, but also including all-round plastic bumper bars painted to match the bodywork.

Comparison rear views of the first-generation XJ-S and post-1991 XJS.

Different treatment to the roofline and rear windows.

By 1995 V12 models were dropped except to special order and the 1996 end-of-line 4.0 litres become known as Celebration models.

The XJS was Jaguar's most successful sporting model up to that time, with as many produced over a 21-year life than all the classic XKs and E-Types together.

NUMBERS PRODUCED: XJ-S (pre-HE): 15,526; XJ-S 5.3-litre coupé: 46,103; XJ-S 5.3-litre cabriolet: 3863; XJ-S 3.6-litre cabriolet: 1150; XJ-S 5.3-litre convertible: 11,571; XJR-S coupé: 448; Face-lift models: XJS 5.3-litre coupé: 1199; XJS 5.3-litre convertible: 3674; XJS 6.0-litre coupé: 774; XJS 6.0-litre convertible: 1787; XJS 4.0-litre coupé: 5667; XJS 4.0-litre convertible: 13,864; XJR-S 6.0-litre coupé: 787; XJR-S 6.0-litre convertible: 50.

PRICES WHEN NEW: XJ-S (pre-HE): £8900; XJ-S 5.3-litre coupé: £18,950; XJ-S 5.3-litre cabriolet: £26,995; XJ-S 3.6-litre cabriolet: £20,756; XJ-S 5.3-litre convertible: £36,000; XJR-S coupé: £35,000; Face-lift models:

A new dashboard incorporated conventional analogue instrumentation.

Another special edition, the Le Mans, commemorated Jaguar's 1988 win. Most special features were on the interior, but this example was fitted with the twin headlamp arrangement, also standard for all cars going to the USA.

XJS 5.3-litre coupé: £43,500; XJS 5.3-litre convertible: £50,600; XJS 6.0-litre coupé: £45,100; XJS 6.0-litre convertible: £52,900; XJS 4.0-litre coupé: £33,400; XJS 4.0-litre convertible: £39,000; XJR-S 6.0-litre coupé: £45,500.

COLOURS: **pre-HE**: Old English White, Tudor White, Dark Blue, British Racing Green, Regency Red, Black, Signal Red, Damson Red, Silver, Silver Frost, Carriage Brown, Squadron Blue, Quarts Blue, Yellow Gold, Cotswold Yellow, Juniper Green, Moroccan Bronze; **1978 to face-lift**: Portland Beige, Cobalt Blue, Racing Green, Claret, Black, Silversand, Sebring Red, Rhodium Silver, Chestnut Brown, Sapphire Blue, Grosvenor Brown, Sable Brown, Coronet Gold, Indigo Blue, Clarendon Blue, Cirrus Grey, Cranberry, Regent Grey, Sage Green, Antelope, Windsor Blue, Steel Blue, Mineral Blue, Claret, Nimbus White, Westminster Blue, Jaguar Racing Green, Grenadier Red, Alpine Green, Arctic

Another update came in 1993 with the fitting of body-coloured bumper bars and alloy trim, along with new ranges of alloy wheels.

The face-lifted model of the Jaguar XJR-S.

Another special edition prepared to order by Jaguar's Special Vehicle Operations Department was the 'Insignia'. A special range of bespoke paint and interior finishes were available for each buyer.

The 'Insignia' badging.

The enhanced and better-quality interior of the very late XJS models, in this case, a convertible.

The final design change to the XJS, seen here in the convertible, now a 2+2 seater.

Rear view of the very late XJS convertible with a different window arrangement in the hood.

Another late example of the XJS interior, in this case, with a conventional clock on the console, rather than the computer in the previous image.

The very 'occasional' rear seating of later convertibles.

Blue, Bordeaux Red, Crimson, Dorchester Grey, Moorland Green, Satin Beige, Silver Birch, Solent Blue, Sovereign Gold, Talisman Silver, Tungsten, Glacier White, Signal Red; **post-face-lift to 1996**: Arctic Blue, Savoy Grey, Diamond Blue, Mica Jade Green, Mica Gunmetal, Mica Regency Red, Brooklands Green, Tuscany Bronze, Meteor Red, British Racing Green, Kingfisher Blue, Platinum, Silver Frost, Oyster, Mica Flamenco, Mica Moroccan Red, Mica Rose Bronze, Sapphire Blue, Titanium, Ice Blue, Topaz, Steel Grey.
TECHNICAL: **Engines**: 5.3-litre (V12): size: 5343cc; cylinders: 12; carb: fuel-injection; bore & stroke: 90mm x 70mm; BHP: 285@5800rpm (Pre-HE), 299@5800rpm (HE).
Gearbox: four-speed manual, floor mounted gear change (Pre-HE only); ratios: 1st 9.94; 2nd 8.85; 3rd 4.26; 4th 3.07; three-speed automatic, centre column mounted change; ratios: low 2.39 (5.3), 2.48 (6.0); intermediate 1.45 (5.3), 1.48 (6.0); top 3.07 (5.3), 1.01 (6.0); direct drive 0.75 (6.0); four-speed automatic, centre column mounted change; low 2.48 (3.6), 3.55 (4.0); intermediate 1.48

Comparison aspect of the first-generation XJ-S alongside the very late XJS.

A last-off-the-line Celebration convertible with the attractive diamond-turned alloy wheels.

An interesting comparison, from right to left: 1970s XJ-S, 1980s XJ-S, and 1990 XJS.

(3.6,) 2.04 (4.0); top 1.01 (3.6), 1.40 (4.0); direct drive 0.75 (3.6), 1.0 (4.0).
Brakes: Girling, ventilated discs all round, servo assisted.
Suspension: front independent semi-trailing double wishbone, coil springs, anti-roll bar. Rear Independent, lower wishbone/upper driveshaft link, radius arms, twin coil springs.
Steering: rack and pinion with power assistance.
Tyres: 205 70VR 15.
DIMENSIONS: **length**: 15ft 11.5 in; **width**: 5ft 10.5in; **height**: 4ft. 1.5in; **wheelbase**: 8ft 6in; **track**: front 4ft 10in; rear 4ft 10.5in; **weight**: 33cwt.

XJ40/X300/X308

The original XJ had been a tremendous success, being the only Jaguar saloon for 19 years, but by the 1980s it was starting to get overtaken by the competition, particularly in technological terms. Jaguar addressed the situation with an entirely new car to carry on the XJ name. Codenamed XJ40, it was launched in 1986 and was given the Car of the Year award for its style and innovation.

A new squarer body style, akin to the fashion of the day, still incorporated features that made it instantly recognisable as a Jaguar. Made from 25 per cent fewer body panels, it was cheaper and easier to build. It incorporated the then-new AJ6 six-cylinder 3.6-litre engine (first seen in the XJ-S) for

The XJ40 heralded a new era for Jaguar's saloon car range from 1986, the most significant and tested model up to that time.

The base model from the early XJ40 period, still known as the XJ6, but with a new body, a unique-to-the-model 2.9-litre engine, and pitched in trim terms to an entry-level market. Note the plastic wheel covers; alloy wheels were an extra-cost option at this time.

An early 3.6-litre Sovereign with the special metric-sized wheels/tyres. Note the different front light treatment to the standard XJ6, although in some markets, even these up-market versions had to have the conventional four-headlamp treatment instead.

Rear view of the early XJ40s with scripted badging and very little chromed adornment.

the top-priced models and a smaller 2.9-litre single camshaft engine (derived from half a V12 unit) for the others. Manual and automatic transmission were available, the latter with a new 'J-gate' selector, unique to Jaguar. New suspension incorporated self-levelling and models were produced as both Jaguars and Daimlers, the latter with a higher state of trim.

Internally, it was again all new, with a digital dashboard and different standards of trim according to model. The most significant changes involved electrics. With all-new technology, this was the most advanced car

Interior of the standard XJ6, in this case with the Getrag manual gearbox and straight grain woodwork and tweed upholstery.

An early high-spec XJ40 with veneer and leather upholstery. Note the push-buttons on the right of the steering wheel, operating the cruise control and on-board basic computer.

The very early Sovereign models had a matt black painted panel to the boot area.

The pre-1990 electronic instrumentation with bar gauges and a Vehicle Condition Monitor Screen to the right.

electronically available on the British market at that time.

In 1990, when Jaguar was sold to Ford, the 3.6-litre engine gave way to a 4.0-litre version and the following year the 2.9-litre engine was deleted and replaced with a 3.2-litre version of the AJ6 unit. The original bodyshell was never designed to take a wider V engine in an attempt by the Jaguar engineers to prevent Rover's V8 unit being fitted during this British Leyland era. Eventually the car was re-engineered to take Jaguar's own V12 engine, now of 6.0 litres capacity, which was launched in 1993.

During the later production of the XJ40 some special editions came about, like the S and Gold, trying to capture a younger audience to the car, and even a limited run of long-wheelbase versions.

Production of the XJ40s came to an end in 1994 to make way for a considerably

The extra rear chrome trim on the later models.

In 1993, Jaguar introduced the V12 XJ40s, identifiable externally by badging, the gold growler in the black grille radiator, four-headlamps, and wider wheels.

With the introduction of the 3.2-litre and 4.0-litre models, extra trim began to appear, and further alloy wheel options, like these Lattice type.

The special edition Gold model with diamond-turned wheels, unique colour schemes.

Special edition 'S' model with five-spoke alloy wheels, additional coachlines and inset plastic panel to the rear boot area.

re-engineered car built with the advantage of Ford money.

Ford looked to improve Jaguar's production, profitability and quality. The first move was a new assembly installed at the Browns Lane Plant. Ford then interrogated the XJ40 saloon, which had always suffered some issues, and also took note of Jaguar's heritage, leading to the XJ40's successor, the X-300: known at the time as the 'New Series XJ'.

The XJ40 was re-engineered into the new XJ using the underpinnings of the previous model, with new inner and outer body panels designed to finer tolerances. The opportunity was taken to add more curvaceousness to the styling, paying tribute to the first XJs.

The interior also came in for revision, using – for the first time – aluminium substrates for the dashboard, clad with wood veneers. Newly designed seats and other trim all contributed to an improved air of quality, fit and finish.

The range of models launched was

Interior of the Gold XJ40 with a different seating pattern and wood veneer. By 1994, Jaguar had fitted a passenger airbag in place of the glove compartment.

The interior of the 'S' model, again with a different seating pattern and wood veneer.

The analogue instrument panel introduced from 1990.

The XJR model introduced with a range of options for the more sporting motorist.

The unique rear styling treatment for the XJ40 XJR model.

extensive and targeted, each with its own trim level and drivetrain setup. Engines were based on the existing 6.0-litre V12 or the fairly new AJ16 six-cylinder, first fitted to the later XJSs. Additionally, the AJ16 engine was also available as the first production supercharged model from Jaguar (the XJR). Suspension setups were different for the more luxurious models like the Sovereign and Daimler, while a stiffer setup and wider wheels were fitted to the more sporty models, with a unique specification for the XJR.

Initially, a single wheelbase was available, but later a longer wheelbase was added for selected models, not least the top-of-the-range Daimler Double Six.

During production, many model changes took place, as well as special editions being made, like the Executive (a base model with extra trim at an attractive price) and the SE (Special Equipment, replacing the high-spec Sovereign).

The complete range of X-300 models was destined for a very short production run, realistically as interim models until Jaguar's new AJ-V8 engine was available, which came about in 1997.

The launch of the XJ8, as it was now called (codenamed X-308), included 3.2-litre and 4.0-litre V8 engines, the latter in both normally-aspirated and supercharged form, along with equivalent other models; not least the Daimler Super V8 (replacing the Double Six). With Jaguar's V12 engine now deleted, it was also the first time in XJ production that there was no six-cylinder-engined model.

Although looking remarkably similar to the X-300 with the majority of the body panels unchanged, the XJ8s incorporated lots of new features. Externally, the radiator was a different shape, new lighting was used at the front, along with a revised bumper and under valance treatment, including chromed bumper blades. Internally, although the dashboard appeared very similar, it was different in many areas, not least the instrumentation, which came from the XK8 sports car (see later chapter).

Jaguar offered Daimler variants of many cars from the 1960s (when they took over the company), this also applying to the XJ40. However, unable to market 'Daimler' models in some countries like the USA, special top-of-the-range Vanden Plas models were available.

One of the rare long-wheelbase XJ40s, in this case fitted with Insignia trim (carried out to special order by Jaguar's Special Vehicle Operations Department). Unique paintwork, wheel trim, and interiors applied.

Comparison of one of the earliest XJ40s on the right, with one of the last produced.

Radiator grilles differentiated the various X-300 models from a standard chrome finish to the first of the mesh grilles, continuing the fluted theme for Daimler models.

The X-300 Sport model with less chrome and amended badging, plus Dimple alloy wheels fitted.

The top-of-the-range X-300 Sovereign model (later re-badged SE), with extensive use of chrome finish and various options of alloy wheels.

Rear treatment of the Sovereign X-300 with chromed trims around the rear lights.

The V8 models continued until 2002 in various forms, finally ending production in advance of their replacement the following year, the X-350.

NUMBERS PRODUCED:
2.9-litre XJ6 (XJ40 all models): 14,148;
3.6-litre XJ6 (XJ40 all models): 82,922;
3.2-litre (XJ6 (XJ40 all models): 21,163;
4.0-litre XJ6 (XJ40 all models): 86,324;
6.0-litre XJ12 (XJ40 all models): 4143;
3.2-litre XJ6 (X-300 all models): 28,040;
4.0-litre XJ6 (X-300 all models): 59,833;

Sport models featured the coloured radiator grille slats.

The first supercharged Jaguar saloon, the XJR in X-300 form, with an initially special Aquamarine colour. Note the wider wheels and tyres, the mesh grille, and colour coordination of trim.

6.0-litre XJ12 (X-300 all models): 4165.
PRICES WHEN NEW:; 2.9-litre XJ6 (XJ40): £16,495; 3.6-litre XJ6 (XJ40): £18,495; 3.2-litre (XJ6 (XJ40): £26,200; 4.0-litre XJ6 (XJ40): £25,200; 3.2-litre XJ6 Sport (XJ40): £29,950; 3.2-litre XJ6 Gold (XJ40): £28,450; 4.0-litre XJ6 Sport (XJ40): £34,950; 4.0-litre XJ6 Gold (XJ40): £28,950; 6.0-litre XJ12 (XJ40): £46,600; 3.2-litre XJ6 (X-300): £28,950; 3.2-litre XJ6 Sport (X-300): £29,950; 4.0-litre XJ6 Sport (X-300): £34,450; 4.0-litre XJR (X-300): £45,450; 4.0-litre XJ6 (X-300): £34,450; 6.0-litre XJ12 (X-300): £53,450.
COLOURS: **XJ40**: Glacier White, Oyster, Signal Red, Black, Regency Red, Westminster Blue, British Racing Green, Kingfisher Blue, Rose Bronze, Flamenco Red, Gunmetal Grey, Morocco Red, Dorchester Grey, Jade Green, Isis Blue, Silver Frost, Sapphire Blue, Diamond Blue, Platinum Grey, Mica Regency Red, Black Cherry, Mica Black Cherry, Meteor Red; **X-300**: Glacier White, Black, Anthracite, British Racing Green, Carnival Red, Cabernet, Sherwood Green, Silver Frost, Topaz, Steel, Turquoise, Aquamarine, Antigua Blue; **X-308**: Spindrift White, Black, British Racing Green, Kingfisher Blue, Signal Red, Westminster Blue, Rose Bronze, Flamenco Red, Morocco Red, Jade Green, Sherwood Green, Silver Frost, Sapphire Blue, Topaz, Ice Blue, Titanium Grey, Steel, Aquamarine, Nautilus Blue, Spruce Brown.

Body style differences between the red XJ6 and Sport, to the long-wheelbase model (the extra length in the rear doors), in this instance an XJ12.

A special edition Executive model incorporated features of the standard XJ6 and Sport features for a limited period.

More of a contrast for Sport X-300 models with the option of part leather/cloth seating with revised shape and pattern, darkened woodwork, and other trim.

Interior of the X-300, looking similar but very different to the previous (XJ40) models. Rounded seats, better-finished wood veneer on metal substrates, better switchgear, and other trim.

TECHNICAL: Engines: 2.9-litre: size: 2919cc; cylinders: six; carb: fuel-injection; bore & stroke: 91mm x 74.8mm; BHP: 165@5600rpm.
3.2-litre: size: 3239cc; cylinders: six; carb: fuel-injection; bore & stroke: 91mm x 83mm; BHP: 200@5250rpm (XJ40) 219@5100rpm (X-300).
3.2-litre: size: 3248cc; cylinders: V8; carb: fuel-injection; bore & stroke: 86mm x 70mm; BHP: 240@6350rpm.
3.6-litre: size: 3590cc; cylinders: six; carb:

The Executive X-300 with Sport seating and other trim from conventional models.

Rear view of the X-308, with new bumper treatment and badging.

The X-308, far more than a facelift X-300, although most body panels remained the same. The whole of the frontal aspects were new.

A direct comparison between the X-300 (on the left) and the X-308. A new bumper design with revised lighting and a restyled radiator grille.

Comparison of rear styling of the X-300 Sport (left) and X-308 Sport. A new bumper bar, and now the chrome boot finisher is body-coloured on the later model.

The X-308 Sport carried over most of the features from the previous model ...

fuel-injection; bore & stroke: 91mm x 92mm; BHP: 221@5000rpm.
4.0-litre: size: 3980cc; cylinders: six; carb: fuel-injection (plus supercharger XJR); bore & stroke: 91mm x 102mm; BHP: 235@4750rpm (XJ40) 249@4800rpm (X-300) 326@5000rpm (XJR).
4.0-litre: size: 3996cc; cylinders: V8; carb: fuel-injection (plus supercharger XJR); bore & stroke: 86mm x 86mm; BHP: 290@6100rpm (370@6150rpm XJR).
6.0-litre (V12): size: 5993cc; cylinders: 12; carb: fuel-injection; bore & stroke: 90mm x 78.5mm; BHP: 318@5400rpm.
Gearbox: five-speed manual, centre console gear change (XJ6 only); four-speed automatic

... with a black finish now to the radiator slats. The chromed headlamp washers in the bumpers were an extra-cost option for the lesser models.

The high-performance XJR X-308 model, now boasting the V8 engine.

The top-of-the-range Jaguar Sovereign XJ8, with an all-chrome grille and window surrounds.

The later 4.0-litre model was an upgrade and a cross between a Sport model and a Sovereign.

The much enhanced interior of the X-308 models with a new dashboard, instrument binnacle, door trims, centre console, and controls.

The X-308 Sport with darkened woodwork and different trim.

The later 4.0-litre model taking styling points from the Sport, as well as the Sovereign models.

(J-gate centre console mounted change XJ6/ XJ12); five-speed automatic (J-gate centre console mounted change (XJ8).
Brakes: ventilated discs all round, servo assisted.
Suspension: front independent twin, anti-dive, coil springs; rear independent, lower transverse wishbones, driveshafts upper link, anti-squat, coil springs.
Steering: rack and pinion with power assistance.
Tyres: 15/16/17in according to model (18in XJR V8).
DIMENSIONS: **length**: 16ft 4in; **width**: 5ft 8in; **height**: 4ft 3in; **wheelbase**: 9ft 4in; **track**: front 4ft 8in; rear 4ft 8in; **weight**: 3968lb (2.9/3.2/4.0) 4134 (XJR X-300) 4354 (V12) 3769lb (XJ8) 3913lb (XJR V8).

XK8/XKR (X-100)

Jaguar's XJS had been an incredible success, but after 21 years in production a new sports model was desperately needed: enter the XK8 (code-named X-100). Conceived in lightning-quick time, the XK8 was a credit to those who designed it, seeing a return to a more curvaceous styling with a frontal area not dissimilar to the 1960s E-Types, an aerodynamic body (although still based on the XJS floorpan), a completely new interior and under the skin, Jaguar's new AJ-V8 4.0-litre engine and other major innovations. The new car was built from 30 per cent fewer panels than the XJS, and was 25 per cent torsionally stiffer.

Introduced in 1996 as a 2+2, in both fixed-head coupé and convertible, the latter with a fully retractable electric roof with heated glass rear screen. To ensure more than adequate luggage space in the boot of the convertible, although the hood completely retracted below the rear deck of the body, a separate tonneau cover had to be fixed over it by the driver.

There were two trim options, Classic using traditional all leather and walnut veneer, and Sports with half leather/cloth trim and dark-stained straight grained veneer. New advanced rubber meant better door and window sealing and the technology included self-closing windows into the seals.

As well as the first use of the new V8 engine, the XK8 incorporated the latest

The 1996 XK8 coupé with its standard-fit 17in Revolver alloy wheels.

The equivalent 1996 XK8 convertible, fitted with the optional 18in fluted wheels.

The early XK8s are identified by the inset fog lights. Chromed 'half moons' in the headlamps are the headlamp washers.

Early XK8s from the rear are identified by the lack of chrome, the shallow rear bumper, and no boot lock button. The key had to be inserted into the 'XK8' badge to open the boot.

An early Sport interior with the darkened wood veneer. The seats (with inclusive headrests) were half cloth/half leather, although all-leather could be specified.

Early XK8 interior, in this instance the 'Classic' style with walnut veneer and all-leather trim.

electronically controlled ZF five-speed automatic transmission and an entirely new aircraft technology front subframe. There was also a revised suspension with the option of Jaguar's new CATS (Computer Active Technology System), plus upgrades to braking and steering.

In 1998 two additional models were added to the range, the coupé and convertible XKR, the first supercharged sports cars from Jaguar. The upgraded 4.0-litre V8 engine was mated to a stronger Mercedes automatic transmission. The XKR had the CATS suspension as standard plus a new Servotronic steering system and upgraded brakes to match the performance. The addition of a mesh radiator grille, cooling louvres set into the bonnet and a discrete spoiler on the boot and new badges segregated the XKR from the XK8. For the first time on any Jaguar, the supercharged models had wider tyres/wheels at the back to the front. Internally the seat trim was amended and even 'supercharged' logos appeared in the main instruments!

Jaguar later introduced a range of

The XKR identifiable by the mesh inset into the nose, badging, and louvres on the bonnet. Phoenix Red (the colour of this car) was the launch colour, initially only available on XKRs but also adopted later for XK8s. The Double-Five alloy wheels were another new item, initially only for the XKR.

The unique XKR badge.

The 2000 Silverstone model, released to coincide with Jaguar's launch into Formula One. All painted Platinum Silver with unique badging. 20in Detroit alloys were standard, and an R-Performance handling kit was fitted with bigger brakes, uprated anti-roll bars and springs, recalibrated steering and shock absorbers. There was also a better sound system and 'Silverstone' identification in the cockpit.

The XKR with the discrete spoiler across the top of the boot lid and the rubber 'lip' added to the rear wheelarches, a legal addition as the wider rear wheels stood slightly proud of the body.

Updated 2001 models with flush-mounted fog lights, slight amendments to the nose splitter bar, a different range of alloy wheels.

R-Performance enhancements for the XKs with larger wheels, brakes, etc. The standard of equipment was increased from 2000 with such items as satellite navigation and adaptive cruise control added.

The first XKR special edition (Silverstone) was also announced with such 100 produced in Platinum Silver and special badging, 20in Detroit split-rim wheels and an ungraded handling package.

Internal and external styling face-lifts took place in 2001, all improvements, not least the fitting of a conventional push-button boot lid release (previously having to use the key.

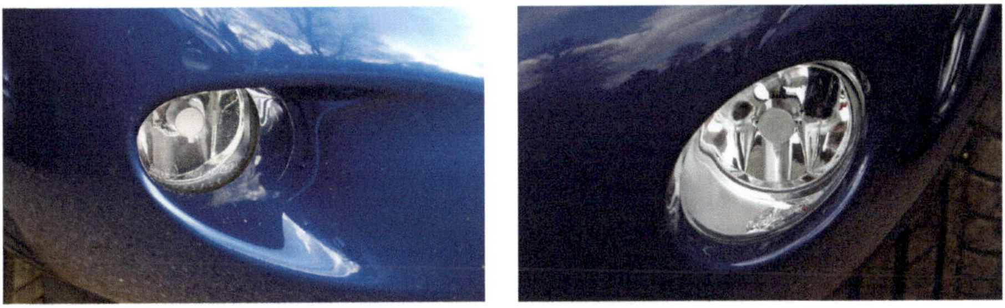

The original inset fog lights and the later flush-mounted from 2001.

At the rear, the original rear lamp units were replaced by this jewelled type with a chromed surround.

The rear of the 2001 model, the boot now having a chromed nacelle incorporated the embossed 'Jaguar' name and a push-button lock to open the lid. The bumper now incorporates an under spoiler that hides more of the underside. Note also the new seating, which now incorporates separately adjustable headrests for the first time.

Extra safety features now included side airbags and reinforced body side members. New seats provided better support and incorporated separated headrests.

Another special edition was announced in 2001, the XKR100 commemorating the centenary of the founder of the company, Sir William Lyons.

For 2002 Jaguar dubbed the updated model as "The new generation Jaguar XK", arguably bringing in the most significant changes to the model since its introduction. The engine was enlarged to 4.2 litres capacity, the Mercedes six-speed transmission was now fitted to all models, there were better brakes, chassis, improved electronics and revised interior trim. Externally smarter badging was applied and the headlamps were fitted with black surround recesses.

Yet another special edition, the Portfolio was introduced for the US market with unique colour schemes and enhanced trim.

In 2004 the XKs were face-lifted again stylistically if not technologically. Exterior styling was made more contemporary and cleaner if not involving any new panelling. New paint finishes, interior trim detailing and veneers all helped refresh the look of the XK.

In the same year another special edition 'Carbon Fibre' was introduced, exclusive to the UK initially with just 100 built. Again based on the XKR, it was marketed as the most well-equipped model with a carbon fibre finished dashboard, and cost £4500 more than the equivalent standard XK8. Proving popular, Jaguar went on to produce a further 200, and the model was released to the US market.

The last models produced in 2005 were

All XK8/Rs had 2+2 seating, trimmed to match the front seats.

The 2001 XKR model.

The XKR 100 (here with its saloon counterpart the XJR). Commemorating the centenary of Sir William Lyons, all these cars were finished in black, an R-Performance handling kit, alloy surrounds to the instrumentation and drilled alloy foot pedals, plus identification plaques.

From 2003, the option of duotone upholstery was available, and note here the fitting of an integrated satellite navigational system in the dashboard (replacing the auxiliary instruments and clock).

From 2003, as well as the mechanical changes identified in the accompanying text, extra equipment was fitted as standard with more options of interior finishes and trim. Note the new 'darkened' headlights.

called 'S' in UK and Europe and 'Victory' in the States, the best finished and detailed cars to complete a superb run from 1996 to 2005.

NUMBERS PRODUCED: XK8 coupé: 19,748; XK8 convertible: 46,760; XKR coupé: 9661; XKR convertible: 13,895.
PRICES WHEN NEW: XK8 coupé: £47,950; XK8 convertible: £54,950; XKR coupé: £60,105; XKR convertible: £67,105.
COLOURS: Spindrift, White Onyx, British Racing Green, Emerald Green, Aquamarine, Sherwood Green, Alpine Green, Seafrost, Sapphire Blue, Westminster Blue, Antigua Blue, Pacific Blue, Adriatic Blue, Amaranth, Ultraviolet, Ice Blue, Zircon Blue, Mistral Blue,

The US Portfolio special edition with a unique colour range ...

... and enhanced duotone interior with heightened wood veneer.

2004 XK8 with its last styling upgrades. The removal of the side rubbing stripe and the addition of the plastic over-sills. Note also the reshaped nose.

The 2004 convertible.

The 2004 XKR front with the new nose and more pronounced mesh grille.

This view of the 2004 car shows the deeper rear bumper with a cover over the tow hitch, the new heater badging, and it emphasises the new oversills.

The 2004 XK8 front (compare to the XKR).

Additional veneer finishes, including a Piano high-gloss black, and the option of Recaro seating for the later models.

Better quality trim available, including for the Recaro seating, and different trim finishes now including carbon fibre.

The carbon fbre model, introduced in 2004. An XKR fitted with most options as standard ...

... naturally including carbon fibre finish to the dashboard and the aluminium instrument surrounds.

Titanium, Meteorite, Platinum, Quartz, Slate, Anthracite, Ebony, Midnight Black, Topaz, Roman Bronze, Carnival Red, Phoenix Red, Salsa Red, Radiance Red.
TECHNICAL: Engines: 4.0-litre: size: 3996cc; cylinders: V8; carb fuel-injection (plus supercharger XKR); bore & stroke: 86mm x 86mm; BHP: 290@4250rpm (370@6150rpm XKR).
4.2-litre: size: 4196cc; cylinder: V8; carb: fuel-injection (plus supercharger XKR); bore & stroke: 96mm x 90.3mm; BHP:

The last of the line models, including the 'Victory' for both coupé and convertible form for the US market and ...

... the same car, identified as the '4.2 S' for others, including the home market.

The last badging on the XK8/R models.

The rear view of the later XKR models, now fitted with quad exhaust tailpipes, and note the revised cleaner badging and deeper bumper.

The first and last off the line, on the right, the first production XK8 coupé from 1996, alongside the 2005 last XKR coupé.

300@6000rpm (400@6100rpm XKR).
Gearbox: five-speed automatic (J-gate centre console mounted change (XK8); six-speed automatic (J-gate centre console mounted change (XKR).
Brakes: ventilated discs all round, servo assisted.
Suspension: front independent double wishbones, anti-dive, coil springs.
Rear Independent, double wishbones, driveshafts upper link, anti-squat, coil springs (CATS selected models).
Steering: rack and pinion with power assistance.
Tyres: 17/18/19/20in according to model.
DIMENSIONS: **length**: 15ft 8in; **width**: 5ft; **height**: 4ft 2.5in; **wheelbase**: 8ft 5in; **track**: front 4ft 7.5in; rear 4ft 7.5in; **weight**: 3560lb (4.0 coupé), 3759lb (4.0 convertible), 3816lb (4.0 XKR coupé), 3814lb (4.0 XKR convertible), 3715lb (4.2 coupé), 3913lb (4.2 convertible), 3825lb (4.2 XKR coupé), 4001lb (4.2 XKR convertible).

S-TYPE

For nearly 30 years Jaguar had only been producing one luxury saloon car, the XJ. Although the XJs had been highly successful, Jaguar had lost market share due to not having any small luxury saloons to counteract the growing competition from the likes of BMW and other manufacturers. Their extended range of cars enabled drivers to get 'on the ladder' and as their position in life and finances improved, so they would retain their brand loyalty and buy other models. A wider range of models might even encourage younger drivers into Jaguar ownership and by economies of scale bring down the overall costs of production.

With all this in mind and past experiences in the 1960s with the Mark 2s and 'S' models, and with the benefits of Ford money and its parts bin, Jaguar looked to introduce a new medium-sized car to compete and re-establish its position of superiority in this area.

Working with Ford and particularly its Lincoln brand in the States, a new model was conceived to be named the S-Type, a

The S-Type, launched in 1999, although all-new, took its title from the namesake 'S' from the 1960s.

The styling was very curvaceous, unlike any other design of Jaguar or competitor, instantly recognisable from the overall sloping radiator grille.

All S-Types had twin exhaust pipes. A substantial part of the rear bodywork was made up of the bumper arrangement, and the chromed boot plinth bore an incredible resemblance to the later plinth on the XK8 models. Only the 4.0-litre model carried an engine badge at the rear at this time.

A very well-proportioned design, smaller than any of the XJs that had been the mainstay of Jaguar saloon production for years. The S-Type had its own unique set of alloy wheels (dependent on model).

throwback to the successful 1960s medium sized model, then just called the 'S'. Using elements of the Ford parts bin alongside Jaguar's in-house engineering and styling expertise, the S-Type, launched in 1999, offered customers a new dimension in Jaguar ownership - a smaller more economical model, at a lower price.

The S-Type was all new and the first complete model to be built at Jaguar's Castle Bromwich (Birmingham) facility. Based on the jointly developed Jaguar/Ford floorpan, also used on Lincoln's LS model, a new curvaceous body was created using the very latest body pressing techniques, a multitude of shapes and body lines were achieved. Amongst these,

The interior layout was different from any other previous (or future) Jaguar models. This is the base model, but with leather upholstery and manual transmission. The centre console area differed according to model specification, in this case with the radio/CD system. Unfortunately, initially, it was fitted inside the glove box, leaving little space for 'gloves'!

The unusual console treatment finished in metal was not to the taste of Jaguar traditionalists. This example has the drawer on the left-hand side, which could be used for storage.

the side of the car was a complete monoside, and Jaguar stated that the bonnet pressing alone was the most complex produced from a single pressing.

A unique style was achieved, modern in design but with a retro-feel, taking cues from the Mark 2 in size and roof curvature, and even the 1950s racing C-Type from its radiator grille design.

Internally, the S-Type was also an all-new package, carrying nothing over from other models.

The S-Type was initially powered by the existing AJ-V8 4.0-litre V8 engine and five-speed automatic transmission (from the XJ and XK) in normally-aspirated form, plus a new

S-Types were initially available with leather or, as here, with cloth trim.

This top-specification model had Jaguar's first on-board integrated satellite navigational system, which could also incorporate a degree of voice activation.

3.0-litre V6 petrol unit, mated to either a Ford based four-speed automatic transmission or Ford five-speed manual gearbox.

S-Types featured a then unique 'swan-neck' front suspension design with also a new rear suspension package with integrated components from the Ford parts bin.

Electronically, the car was very advanced, which could be fitted with the option of an integrated satellite navigation system and even voice activation.

Internally, the S-Type was an entirely new design with a more modern approach to layout and style. Less wood veneer, choice

With this early dashboard, an owner could also specify an integrated phone system for the first time. This is the holder for ease of use.

The Sport model with colour-coded exterior trim.

Rear view of the Sport model, showing the lack of chrome.

The new interior from 2002, the most significant parts being the revised seat design and the whole centre console area.

The first update for the S-Type came in 2002 with a new bonnet, radiator grille (incorporating a growler badge), and the deletion of the side rubbing stripes.

of heating/air-conditioning systems, steering wheel mounted controls and much more. Somewhat avant-garde to many traditional Jaguar buyers, this new design would not last long!

The car was an instant success with 70,000 sold in the first year and, as intended, it started to open up a new market for Jaguar, even if at the point of launch, Rover came out with its all new '75' model, in many ways hitting the same market.

In 2001 an extra model was added to the range taking note of a similar approach made with the XJs, the Sport. With the replacement of chrome trim with body coloured finish, different seating, dark stained maple wood veneer and other minor trim changes.

For 2002, however, there were major

The various designs of the centre console from 2002 dependent on car specification, from the basic heating system, through air-conditioning, and full sat nav system.

changes with more new models and an internal face-lift. Due to the mixed reaction to the layout, the dashboard and other trim were re-designed to the same style as the then recently introduced small saloon, the X-Type and the shortly to be announced new XJ (see later sections).

There were a few minor exterior trim changes, along with more efficient laser welding of the bodywork and higher-strength steels used for better rigidity.

Mechanically, new, additional engines were added, a 2.5-litre version of the V6 unit, the enlargement of the V8 to 4.2 litres capacity and a supercharged version of that engine providing the high-performance model, the S-Type R. Jaguar's new Mercedes supplied six-speed transmission also became available for the V8 engines.

Further changes took place with a face-lift in 2004 with a lighter aluminium bonnet, revised bumper treatment, a restyle for the

Performance S-Type R, introduced in 2002, with its mesh grille and new bumper design.

The revised frontal treatment, post-2002, of the normally-aspirated models.

The later S-Type with its enhanced interior for the traditional models ...

... or the option of a sportier interior with duotone upholstery and different finishes, like this aluminium trim.

rear and removal of the side rubbing strips, plus new door mirrors.

The biggest change was the addition of yet another new engine, Jaguar's first diesel, the 2.7-litre V6, jointly developed with Peugeot/Citroën. The following year the 2.5-litre engine models were discontinued and the first limited edition XS was announced in 2006, with a sportier look to bumper bars and spoiler.

In 2007, revision to the model range included the Spirit replacing the base model, although better equipped with leather and automatic transmission as standard. All models took on the S-Type R frontal styling. The final S-Type left production later that year.

The S-Type was a very successful model range for Jaguar providing a valuable alternative to the larger XJ.

NUMBERS PRODUCED: 2.5-litre S-Type (all models): 21,765; 3.0-litre S-Type (all models): 172,791; 2.7-litre S-Type (all models): 31,119; 4.0-litre S-Type (all models): 40,058; 4.2-litre S-Type (all models): 27,654.
PRICES WHEN NEW: 2.5-litre S-Type: £24,950; 3.0-litre S-Type: £26,700; 2.7-litre

The revised styling from 2004 with the more assertive frontal treatment, in this case, the S-Type R model.

Early S-Type on the right and later facelift on the left.

S-Type: £29,347; 4.0-litre S-Type: £35,350; 4.2-litre S-Type:£36,000.
COLOURS: Spindrift White, Pacific Blue, Seafrost, Anthracite, Titanium Grey, British Racing Green, Emerald Green, Topaz, Carnival Red, Sapphire Blue, Mistral, Meteorite Silver, Alpine Green, Westminster Blue, Platinum Grey, White Onyx, Roman Bronze, Slate Grey, Quartz, Aspen Green, Zircon, Ebony, Jaguar Racing Green, Adriatic Blue, Midnight, Ultraviolet Blue, Radiance Red, Indigo, Winter Gold.
TECHNICAL: Engines: 2.5-litre: size: 2497cc; cylinders: V6; carb: fuel-injection; bore & stroke: 81.65mm x 79.5mm; BHP: 201@6800rpm.

The revised rear end styling from 2002: the car on the left is one of the normally-aspirated models, the one on right the S-Type R with its unique boot spoiler.

The special edition XS, created near the end of production, featured enhanced trim and a marginally more aggressive look to the exterior.

2.7-litre: size: 2720cc; cylinders: V6; carb: diesel fuel-injection; bore & stroke: 81mm x 86mm; BHP: 206@4000rpm.
3.0-litre: size: 2967cc; cylinders: V6; carb: fuel-injection; bore & stroke: 89mm x 79.5mm; BHP: 240@6800rpm.
4.0-litre: size: 3996cc; cylinders: V8; carb: fuel-injection; bore & stroke: 86mm x 86mm; BHP: 281@6100rpm.
4.2-litre: size: 4196cc; cylinder: V8; carb: fuel-injection (plus supercharger 'R'); bore & stroke: 96mm x 90.3mm; BHP: 300@6000rpm (400@6100rpm ('R').
Gearbox: five-speed all-synchromesh manual gearbox (2.5/3.0 litre); five-speed automatic (J-gate centre console mounted change (2.5/3.0/4.0 litre); six-speed automatic (J-gate centre console mounted change (2.7/4.2 litre).
Brakes: ventilated discs all round, servo assisted.
Suspension: front independent double wishbones, alloy control arms, anti-dive, coil springs; rear independent, double wishbones, alloy control arms, co-axial coil springs (CATS optional).
Steering: rack and pinion with power assistance.
Tyres: 17/18in according to model.
DIMENSIONS: **length**: 15ft 7.5in; **width**: 5ft 7.5in; **height**: 4ft 6in; **wheelbase**: 9ft 4in; **track**: front 5ft; rear 5ft; **weight**: 3572lb (2.5), 3947lb (2.7), 3610lb (3.0), 3805lb (4.0), 3826lb (4.2), 3969lb ('R').

X-TYPE

After the 1999 launch of the S-Type filled one gap in Jaguar's saloon car offering, attention turned to yet another even smaller model, the X-Type. With this car Jaguar hoped to gain a major foothold in the very competitive market held by the likes of BMW's 3 Series. This was entirely new territory for Jaguar, launched under the banner of "The New Jag Generation" in the hope of attracting those who had never previously considered owning a Jaguar, particularly those under 40.

Designed and built during the Ford ownership era, again, like the S-Type, it would rely on their parts bin and in particular aspects of the Mondeo, although still importantly taking advantage of Jaguar expertise in styling, luxury, ride, handling and engineering. Ford involvement meant a speedy process in development leading to an early launch of the model in 2001, only two years after the medium sized S-Type.

The X-Type was the first Jaguar to be built outside of the West Midlands, at the Ford plant on Merseyside which had been refitted especially for this model.

The body styling resembled Jaguar's flagship XJ with the shallow radiator grille and four-headlamp treatment. Because of its smaller dimensions, the roof line was raised to increase interior accommodation and the

The X-Type, although aimed at a different market, took many of its styling cues from the larger XJ.

As was Jaguar's usual practice in those days, various states of external trim were treated differently according to the model. This Sport model had the colour-coded grille surround ...

... whereas this SE model had chrome.

Trim throughout the initial range changed little except for the addition or deletion of chrome.

Jaguar proudly announced that its small saloon had all-wheel drive.

slightly higher rear line of the body provided for a reasonably sized luggage area. The X-Type also benefited from features first seen on the S-Type, like the bumper bar treatment and the latest body pressing technology.

The interior design was new, which would set the scene for the later S-Type models and still to come new XJ. Luxuriously appointed, even for the base model, it, like the exterior styling, was typically quality Jaguar.

Mechanically the X-Type was initially fitted with the 2.5-litre V6 or 3.0-litre V6 petrol engines with five-speed manual or automatic transmissions, from the S-Type. The major difference however, was that the X-Type was the first Jaguar to be equipped with all-wheel-drive, a strong selling point over the

Internally, the X-Type followed Jaguar's practice with luxury touches and a layout that would be standardised with the later S-Type. Seat styling depended on the model, with the usual cars like this ...

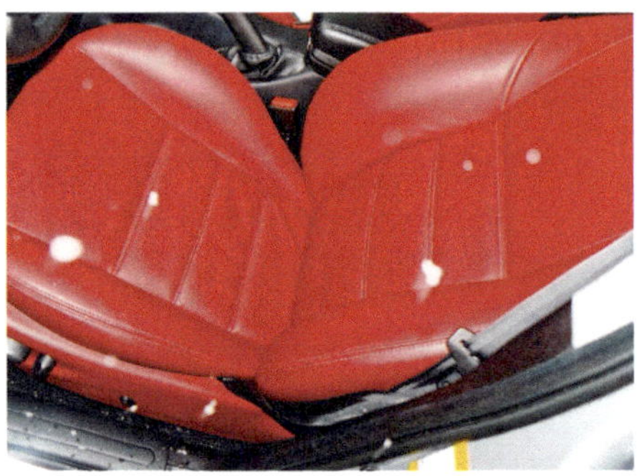

... and sport models having different stitching.

The Indianapolis model was an early special edition featured at the motor show in this launch colour of Ultraviolet.

The interior finish of an Indianapolis model featured an enhanced range of equipment.

The Sport model, with its colour coding, helped attract a younger ownership.

The launch of Jaguar's first production estate car, in the form of the X-Type, was a major boost to sales. It was a very well-proportioned and executed design.

opposition. Steering and suspension followed S-Type practice.

There was just one design (a conventional three-box saloon) available in five models, 2.5-litre Classic, 2.5-litre Sport, 2.5-litre SE (Special Equipment(, 3.0-litre Sport and 3.0-litre SE, and at a starting price of just £22,000, the X-Type represented excellent value for money. Although even the Classic offered all-wheel-drive and air conditioning, an owner didn't get leather upholstery and other luxuries associated with the Jaguar name. The Sport came with colour coordinated trim (instead of chrome), revised interior and again a lesser standard of trim compared to the top of the range SE.

In 2002 an additional engine was offered, a 2.0-litre V6 version of the 2.5-litre unit but

The estate managed to retain elements of the saloon car styling, so it was easily recognisable as a Jaguar.

The two-stage opening of the tailgate, although not unique to the car, was another good selling point for estate car users.

only with front (two-wheel-drive). This opened up another sales opportunity at a lower price point of £19,995 and the engine capacity also helped the model fit into the business bracket for tax advantages.

In the same year at the British Motor Show, Jaguar introduced its first X-Type special edition, the Indianapolis. Only available with the larger V6 engines, it was equipped with luxury features as standard and just three colour schemes. A year later, another new engine joined the range: a 2.0-litre diesel (front-wheel drive), the first Jaguar production car to be fitted with an oil engine.

Another first for Jaguar came in 2004, with the introduction of the X-Type estate car in all engine sizes, the larger engine cars also with all-wheel-drive. A particularly attractive style with some excellent features like the two-piece tailgate and a host of extra cost options, the estate was a winner, again opening up new sales opportunities.

Yet another new engine was announced in 2005, a 2.2-litre diesel (front-wheel drive) available for all models, available with a new six-speed manual transmission as well.

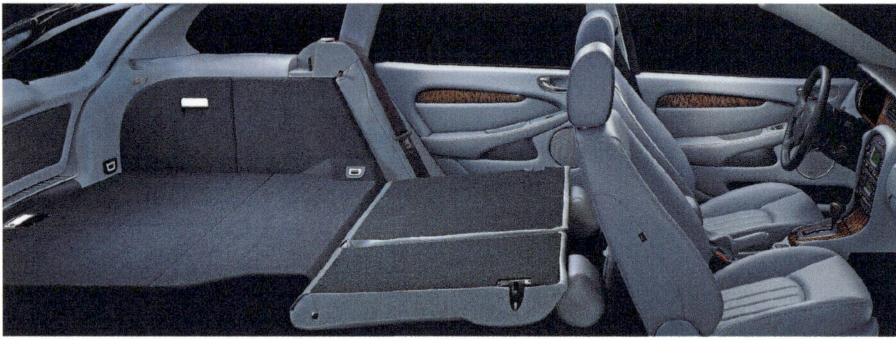

The X-Type estate was an excellent load-lugger with a range of seat options.

Jaguar offered an extensive range of accessories specifically for the estate.

With the Jaguar name, an economical range of engines and trims, and the advantage of all-wheel drive on many models, the X-Type was an ideal workhorse or leisure vehicle, ideally suited to poor weather conditions.

In 2006 Jaguar the Spirit models replaced the basic range and a special edition, the XS offered enhanced standard trim.

In 2007 the X-Type range was face-lifted with styling changes at the front and rear, following similar practice with its larger brother the XJ. By this time the 2.0-litre and 2.5-litre engines had been discontinued.

The last X-Types left production in 2008 coinciding with the S-Type, both to be replaced by a new single model, the XF. The X-Type was an incredibly successful model for Jaguar with over a third of a million being produced.

NUMBERS PRODUCED: 2.0-litre X-Type petrol saloons (all models): 49,762; 2.0-litre X-Type petrol estates (all models): 1587; 2.0-litre X-Type diesel saloons (all models): 55,615; 2.0-litre X-Type diesel estates (all models):

The launch of the diesel X-Type saw some minor changes to the car's exterior look, which were carried over to the other models

The addition of the 2.2-litre engine and six-speed gearbox came with a variety of trim options. Note the different seat material in this example.

The X-Type received a final face-lift nearing the end of production, with numerous changes to both the exterior and interior trims.

The face-lifted estate model.

16,747; 2.2-litre X-Type diesel saloons/estates (all models): 31,294; 2.5-litre X-Type petrol saloons (all models): 99,939; 2.5-litre X-Type petrol estates (all models): 4306; 3.0-litre X-Type petrol saloons (all models): 91,595; 3.0-litre X-Type petrol estates (all models): 4382.

PRICES WHEN NEW: 2.0-litre X-Type petrol

The most noticeable difference in the face-lifted model was the front, with new bumpers, badging, and radiator grille.

Rear view with a smoother, restyled bumper arrangement, and a full-width chrome finisher on the boot.

saloon: £19,995; 2.0-litre X-Type petrol estate: £20,447; 2.0-litre X-Type diesel saloon: £19,995; 2.0-litre X-Type diesel estate: £20,472; 2.2-litre X-Type diesel saloon: £22,302; 2.2-litre X-Type diesel estate: £23,472; 2.5-litre X-Type petrol saloon: £22,000; 2.5-litre X-Type petrol estate: £23,202; 3.0-litre X-Type petrol saloon:

The sleek boot spoiler on the Sport model.

Late face-lifted model with a wider choice of interior finishes.

£25,500; 3.0-litre X-Type petrol estate: £27,052.

COLOURS: White Onyx, Pacific Blue, Phoenix Red, Anthracite, Titanium Grey, British Racing Green, Emerald Green, Topaz, Carnival Red, Adriatic Blue, Westminster Blue, Platinum Grey, Quartz, Ebony, Zircon, Jaguar Racing Green, Ultraviolet Blue, Radiance Red, Salsa Red, Midnight, Indigo, Winter Gold, Glacier Blue, Shadow Grey, Liquid Silver, Chilli Red, Ultimate Black, Emerald Fire, Tekite Grey, Lazuli Blue, Ionian Blue, Porcelain.

TECHNICAL: Engines: 2.0-litre: size: 2099cc; cylinders: V6; carb: fuel-injection; bore & stroke: 81.6mm x 66.8mm; BHP: 157@6800rpm.

2.0-litre: size: 1998; cylinders: V6; carb diesel fuel-injection; bore & stroke: 86mm x 86mm; BHP: 128@3800rpm.

2.2-litre: size: 2198cc; cylinders: V6; carb

The choice of interior trim was extensive on the later X-Types, with some featuring fashionable quilted upholstery at the time.

The evolving design of the X-Type, with the face-lifted model on the left.

diesel fuel-injection; bore & stroke: 86mm x 94.6mm; BHP: 155@3500rpm.
2.5-litre: size: 2495cc; cylinders: V6; carb: fuel-injection; bore & stroke: 81.65mm x 79.5mm; BHP: 194@6800rpm.
3.0-litre: size: 2967cc; cylinders: V6; carb: fuel-injection; bore & stroke: 89mm x 79.5mm; BHP: 231@6800rpm.
Gearbox: five-speed all-synchromesh manual gearbox (2.0/2.5/3.0 litre).
Six-speed all-synchromesh manual gearbox (2.2 litre).
Five-speed automatic (J-gate centre console mounted change (2.0/early 2.5/3.0 litre).
Six-speed automatic (J-gate centre console mounted change (2.2/late 2.5/3.0 litre).
Brakes: ventilated discs all round, servo assisted.
Suspension: front independent double wishbones, alloy control arms, anti-dive, coil springs; rear independent, double wishbones, alloy control arms, co-axial coil springs.
Steering: rack and pinion with power assistance.
Tyres: 16/17/18in according to model.
DIMENSIONS: **length**: 15ft 2.5in (saloons) 15ft 5in (estates); **width**: 5ft 6.6in; **height**: 4ft 4in (saloons) 4ft 8in (estates); **wheelbase**: 8ft 6in; **track**: front 5ft; rear 5ft; **weight**: 3197lb (2.0-litre petrol), 3311 (2.0-litre diesel), 3473lb (2.2 litre), 3428lb (2.5), 3428 (3.0).

X-350

Jaguar had sold over one million XJs over four model ranges since the introduction of the first car to carry that insignia in 1968. The last design's styling origins were back in 1994, and some aspects went back even further, so Jaguar had to address this with this yet another new XJ to remain competitive.

Jaguar at the turn of the century had initiated new manufacturing processes to create mass-produced body panels in aluminium, making the cars lighter, more economical to run, improving longevity and with advantages to the environment. The culmination of this came with the introduction of the next generation XJ, code-named X-350, in 2003.

Concerned not to affect sales to existing XJ customers, the new car was styled remarkably similarly to the outgoing model, and that disguised the major leap forward in technology. The whole body structure was of high-grade aluminium featuring sophisticated

The 2003 XJ6 (X-350) showed a strong resemblance to its predecessor but had a great presence and size. This is the base XJ6 saloon with its somewhat 'egg crate'-style chromed grille.

The Sport model with the matte black grille insert and body-coloured surround.

bonding and self-riveting process. The whole car was significantly lighter (40%) and stiffer (60%) than the outgoing model.

More new technology included air suspension, dynamic stability control, the latest developments of Jaguar's CATS suspension (from the XK sports car), an extensive multi-media system and even a heated steering wheel!

Mechanically, the new XJ used version of Jaguar's existing petrol engines: the 3.0-litre V6 (as fitted to the S-Type), the 4.2-litre V8

The XJR with body-coloured grille surround, and, now common to Jaguar supercharged cars, a mesh grille. Note the different alloy wheel styles between models; a wealth of different versions became available throughout the XJ's production.

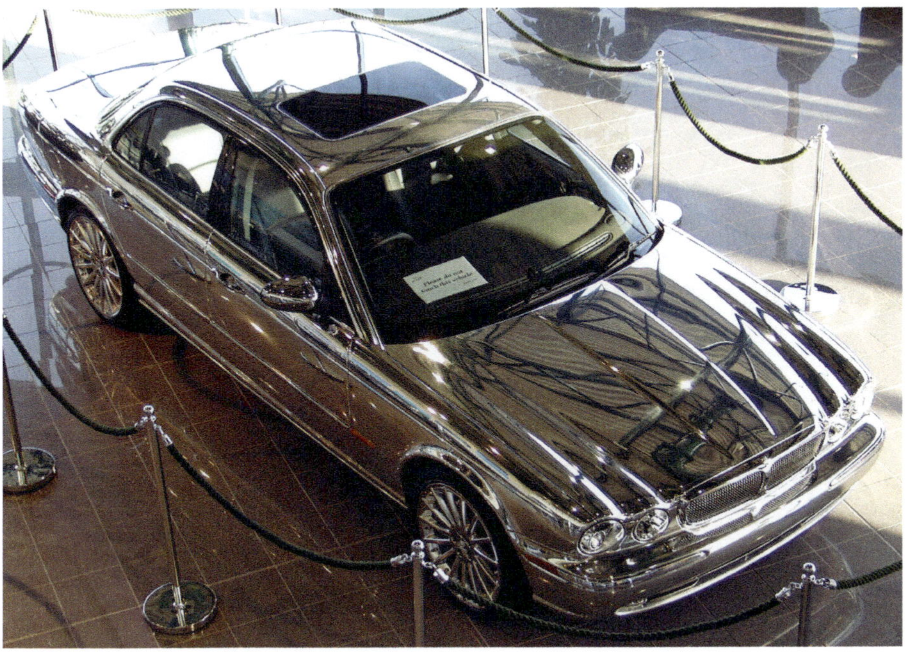

The all-aluminium construction of the XJ was shown off well by this launch model, left in polished metal without paint.

The old (X-308) on the left, alongside the new (X-350), clearly shows the size difference.

Style and size comparisons for the Sport models from the X-308 predecessor (red car) and the X-350.

Quality was the key word for the interior of the X-350, as this SE model shows.

Unique badging for the Jaguar Super V8.

Although this model looks just like the base XJ6 and even the higher-spec SE, it is, in fact, the top of the range Super V8, the only discernible difference being the special wheels and centre covers and rear badging. Internally, it was a very different story as the best-equipped Jaguar model at the time.

in both normally-aspirated and supercharged form (as fitted to the XK) and a new 3.5-litre derived from the other V8, all mated to the existing six-speed automatic transmission.

The interior was essentially styled around Jaguar's 'corporate' look from the later S-Type and X-Types, but with even more luxurious touches and equipment levels, and was arguably of the highest quality yet achieved by the brand.

At initial launch there were no fewer than 10 variants, the XJ6, Sport and SE (Special Equipment) with the 3.0-litre engine, the same combination for the XJ8 with the 3.5-litre engine, two XJ8s with the 4.2-litre engine (Sport and SE) and two supercharged cars (XJR and a new Super V8, at the time replacing a Daimler badged model).

The models and names changed several times during production, in 2004 an extra Sport Premium 3.5-litre V8 was offered with a higher specification than the Sport, a year later made available with the other engines.

From left to right, XJ6, Sport, and XJR.

The rear view shows the new style quality badging, the first time there had been an XJ6 since 1997!

At this point, longer wheelbase models were available on the standard, SE and Super V8.

In 2005 Jaguar's new 2.7-litre V6 diesel engine was added to the range in the Executive (replacing the standard XJ6), Sovereign and Sport Premium models. At the same time the Sport and SE models were discontinued.

A year later a rare special edition Portfolio model was launched, based on a concept for the US market.

As with other Jaguar saloons, the XJ received a face-lift in 2007 with styling changes front and rear and minor trim updates. This included a rationalisation of the models. The 3.5-litre engine was dropped, and what was the SE became the Sovereign. In 2008 this XJ model was finally discontinued

The SE was renamed the Sovereign and featured a chrome finisher on the boot lid.

With the announcement of the 2.7-litre diesel engine model, very little had changed except for direct bonding the front and rear screens (without a finishing surround) and the removal of the side rubbing strips.

in advance of its replacement, yet another XJ, code-named X-351.

Jaguar was happy to announce it had a diesel XJ.

NUMBERS PRODUCED: 2.7-litre XJ6 diesel short wheelbase (all models): 7860; 2.7-litre XJ6 diesel long-wheelbase (all models): 230; 3.0-litre XJ6 short wheelbase (all models): 9999; 3.0-litre XJ6 long-wheelbase (all models): 2709; 3.5-litre XJ8 short wheelbase (all models): 6141; 3.5-litre XJ8 long-wheelbase (all models): 225; 4.2-litre XJ8 short wheelbase (all models): 26,546; 4.2-litre XJ8 long-wheelbase (all models): 17,443; 4.2-litre Supercharged short wheelbase: (all models): 8625; 4.2-litre Supercharged long-wheelbase: (all models): 3082.

PRICES WHEN NEW:; 3.0-litre XJ6: £39,000; 3.5-litre XJ6: £41,550; 2.7-litre XJ6: £43,272; 4.2-litre XJ8: £51,500; 4.2-litre Super V8: £68,500.

Colours: White Onyx, Jaguar Racing Green, British Racing Green, Radiance Red, Pacific Blue, Platinum Grey, Quartz, Ultraviolet Blue,

A varied array of trim finishes and upholstery provided a wider choice for buyers, from contrast piping to two-tone leather.

The longer wheelbase was obtained by extending the floorpan and rear doors to allow for extra legroom in the rear compartment.

Comparison rear compartment space between the normal wheelbase and longer wheelbase models (the latter a Super V8 with a rear compartment entertainment system).

Above and below: A short wheelbase Sport Premium interior with two-tone upholstery and a Super V8 (long-wheelbase), with a rear entertainment system and ruched leather.

The Portfolio which, from a concept, turned into a limited special edition.

Unique features of the Portfolio with individual rear seating and bespoke trim.

Seafrost, Slate, Topaz, Ebony, Zircon, Midnight, Winter Gold, Indigo, Botanical Green, Emerald Fire, Vapour Grey, Frost Blue, Blue Prism, Azure Blue, Ultimate Black, Pearl Grey, Lunar Grey, Liquid Silver, Porcelain, Garnet.

TECHNICAL: Engines: 2.7-litre: size: 2720cc; cylinders: V6; carb diesel fuel-injection; bore & stroke: 81mm x 88mm; BHP: 204@4000rpm.

3.0-litre: size: 2967cc; cylinders: V6; carb: fuel-injection; bore & stroke: 89mm x 79.5mm; BHP: 240@6800rpm.

3.5-litre: size: 3555cc; cylinders: V6; carb: fuel-injection; bore & stroke: 86mm x 76.5mm; BHP: 262@6250rpm.

The front wing side vents on the Portfolio were apparently hewn from solid ingots of aluminium.

4.2-litre: size: 4196cc; cylinder: V8; carb: fuel-injection (plus supercharger); bore & stroke: 86mm x 90.3mm; BHP: 300@6000rpm (400@6100rpm (supercharged).

The 2007 face-lift XJ with its more assertive frontal view, revised wheels, and the addition of front wing side vents in body colour.

Emphasising the new frontal approach to the face-lifted XJ. The mesh grille and body-coloured surround were now common to all Jaguar XJ models.

The front side wing vent appeared on several new Jaguar models afterward.

The face-lift rear with a discrete boot spoiler, full-width chrome finisher (still body-coloured on sportier models), and the new style script for badges.

Face-lift Sovereign interior with minor new touches like the chrome finish to more switchgear, better-figured veneer.

Different approach to interior wood veneer, the addition of aluminium finish instead of wood and bolder seat bolster support – all part of the late XJ range.

As with previous XJs, there were always Daimler versions, not part of this publication, but it's worth mentioning that it was never planned to have a Daimler X-350 until requests from previous owners prompted a limited run to special order.

Outside the home market, the trend of using the Vanden Plas name continued, even with these later XJs; this Super V8/Daimler specified model was known in the States as the Vanden Plas!

Gearbox: six-speed automatic (J-gate centre console mounted change.
Brakes: ventilated discs all round, servo assisted.
Suspension: front independent double wishbones, anti-dive, coil springs and air suspension; rear independent, double wishbones, coil springs and air suspension.
Steering: rack and pinion with power assistance.
Tyres: 17/18/19in according to model.
DIMENSIONS: **length**: 16ft 6in; **width**: 6ft 08in; **height**: 4ft 7in (swb), 4ft 7.7in (lwb); **wheelbase**: 9ft 7.5in; **track**: front 5ft 08in; rear 5ft; **weight**: 3657lb (2.7 swb); 3671lb (2.7 lwb); 3395lb (3.0 swb), 3407lb (3.0 lwb); 3547lb (3.5 swb), 3560lb (3.5 lwb); 3547lb (4.2 swb), 3560lb (4.2 lwb); 3671 (supercharged).

XK/XKR (X-150)

Jaguar's 'new' XK sports car was announced in October 2005 for the 2006 model year. The car stemmed from a concept released by Jaguar called the ALC (Aluminium Lightweight Coupé) that had been well received. Perhaps for the first time, a concept car had been pretty well faithfully transformed into a production sports car as the New XK (as it became known, code-named X-150) was launched. The new car not only inherited its name from the previous model (without the '8'), but gained the aluminium technology that had been used on the contemporary XJ saloon (X-350).

The entirely new body and architecture owed nothing to the previous XK, built entirely from aluminium, it was lighter (by 20 per cent), stiffer (by 50 per cent), more aerodynamic, and economical to maintain and run, and with a contemporary 'sharper' style. The car was designed as a 2+2 convertible first, then the coupé was added, which helped build in the stiffness of the monocoque. It was Jaguar's first convertible to have a fully retractable electric hood that folded away beneath a metal tonneau cover, providing a clean line to the bodywork.

The car was packed with features innovative for the day, including keyless entry and start, active front lighting, sequential gearshift from steering wheel mounted paddles, automatically deployed roll-over bars in case of accident and a pyrotechnic deployable bonnet system in case of contact with a pedestrian.

Mechanically, the new XK used the existing 4.2-litre V8 engine and gearbox from the previous model, and like its predecessor, initially only normally aspirated. It would be another year before the new XKR was launched. A small run of about 1300 cars was also produced with the X-350 3.5-litre V8 engine, specifically for tax-conscious markets.

The steering and suspension were modified aspects from other Jaguar models, although without air suspension. Larger brakes incorporated a four-channel ABS system and electronic distribution to ensure an even balance of brake force across all wheels. A key feature of the new model was the sound produced, via a valve system, which not only sounded good from the outside, but allowed a degree of 'comfortable' sporting noise to enter the interior.

The interior was also completely new, with a much deeper dashboard, instrument layout and integrated infotainment system with satellite navigation as standard. Other standard features included a choice of three trim finishes, air-conditioning and cruise control.

Jaguar ALC (Aluminium Lightweight Coupé) concept released prior to the X-150 on which the New XK was to be based.

The old versus the new. The outgoing XK8 coupé and the New XK coupé at the press launch in South Africa.

The New XK was much more assertive in styling, yet still retained the basic look of the older model.

The convertible was a vital market for the New XK, and to eliminate issues that many topless cars experience, the X-150 was designed to be one, instead of the usual practice of developing a coupé and then converting it.

The New XK coupé was particularly attractive, more so because of the pronounced 'haunch' over the rear wheels.

A very clean new look to the front and unlike the XK8 (X-100), there was no longer a need for a registration plate to obscure the mouth. The unusual light unit included directional bulbs which turned with the steering.

Just the two cars formed the launch, the XK convertible and coupé, followed in 2007 by the two same bodies with the 4.2-litre supercharged engine. With increased performance due to the light body, the steering and CATS suspension were upgraded and the XKR was now achieving 420bhp. Subtle styling changes and interior trim separated the XKR from the XK.

During 2007 and 2008, minor changes to

the model took place, and Jaguar introduced the Portfolio model (different to the later Portfolio XK now covered in this book). Only available as a coupé in black paint for the US or silver in the UK with an alloy finished grille, vents and bonnet louvres (different to the XKR). It also had an enlarged braking system.

In 2008 came another special edition: the XKR-S (again different to a later XK with the same name), with a recalibrated engine management system, suspension and aerodynamic improvements, and the uprated brakes from the Portfolio already mentioned. Jaguar claimed a top speed of 174mph,

Jaguar had achieved a very purposeful rear style, and in the coupé, there was significant luggage space available. The New XK is shown here against one of its successful predecessors, the E-Type.

A very different approach was made to the designing of the interior, and quality was the keyword. Standard equipment included satellite navigation, push-button starting, and steering wheel-mounted paddles. With such sophisticated technology, there was no longer a need for auxiliary instruments like oil pressure, battery condition, or even temperature! Despite its modernity, traditional walnut veneer was the favoured option for many buyers, although ...

... a more contemporary burr elm was available ...

... or an aluminium finish.

With the hood of the convertible now disappearing below a metal tonneau panel that automatically raised and lowered during the operation, it left the car with a completely flat rear deck. The two defined rectangular areas in the cover hide the roll-over bars which automatically deploy in case of the vehicle turning over.

making it the fastest production Jaguar ever produced at the time. Just 200 of the model were produced for European sale only.

At the same time, Jaguar introduced an exterior styling pack that could be fitted by dealerships and painted to match the car. This involved the fitting of a new front nose and rear bumper and tailpipes.

Also in 2008, a little confusingly, Jaguar announced the XK50 to replace the original normally-aspirated XK. This model had extra standard equipment like 20in alloy wheels, enhanced front and rear body trim like the earlier styling kit, plus some aluminium additions to the interior. Even more confusingly, from this the XK60 was created to commemorate the 60th anniversary of Jaguar's famous XK120 sports car. Apart from the body enhancements, the front wings vents were chromed with bright upper and lower front grille meshes.

The XKs remained in production until 2009 when the models were substantially upgraded with a new 5.0-litre V8 engine plus many other significant changes, including some styling enhancements. The XKs continued in production until 2014.

A significant moment for Jaguar as the very first New XK rolled off the production lines at their Castle Bromwich factory, alongside its sports car predecessor the E-Type, and from Jaguar's racing heritage, the D-Type.

The body kit Jaguar designed for the XK, which later was adopted for the special edition commemorative edition.

NUMBERS PRODUCED: XK 3.5-litre (all models): 1300; XK 4.2-litre coupé: (all models): 9434; XK 4.2-litre convertible (all models): 10,406; XKR 4.2-litre coupé (all models): 6310; XKR 4.2-litre convertible (all models): 5256.
PRICES WHEN NEW: XK 3.5-litre coupé: £59,232; XK 3.5-litre convertible: £65,232; XK 4.2-litre coupé: £59,232; XK 4.2-litre convertible: £65,232; XKR 4.2-litre coupé: £66,732; XKR 4.2-litre convertible: £72,732; XKR 4.2-litre Portfolio coupé: £75,597; XKR 4.2-litre Portfolio convertible: £78,232; XKR-S 4.2-litre coupé: £79,995; XK60 4.2-litre coupé: £60,995; XK60 4.2-litre convertible: £66,995.
COLOURS: British Racing Green, Jaguar Racing Green, White Onyx, Porcelain, Seafrost, Liquid Silver, Lunar Grey, Quartz, Slate Grey, Vapour Grey, Pearl Grey, Zircon, Frost Blue,

The styling changes (including exhaust tailpipes) for the kit, which became the XK 50.

The first-generation Portfolio model with brightly finished front wing vents and quad exhaust tailpipes.

The XKR models came a year after the XK with various exterior trim changes.

The XKR-s revised mesh grilles and modified side lighting.

Rear view of the XKR with satin finished boot finisher, deeper under-bumper, and quad exhaust tailpipes.

To aid cooling from the more powerful engine, XKRs featured these stylish bonnet louvres.

Interior of the XKR with the stiffer bolsters to the seats and alloy trim.

Ultraviolet Blue, Blue Prism, Azure Blue, Indigo, Midnight, Ebony Black, Salsa Red, Radiance Red, Winter Gold, Celestial Black, Ultimate Black, Botanical Green. Emerald Fire.

TECHNICAL: Engines: 3.5-litre: size: 3555cc; cylinders: V6; carb: fuel-injection; bore & stroke: 86mm x 76.5mm; BHP: 262@6250rpm.

4.2-litre: size: 4196cc; cylinders: V8; carb: fuel-injection (plus supercharger); bore & stroke: 86mm x 90.3mm; BHP: 298@6000rpm (420@6250rpm (supercharged).

Gearbox: six-speed automatic sequential change (J-gate and paddle control).

Brakes: ventilated discs all round, servo assisted.

Suspension: front independent unequal

length wishbones, coil springs; rear independent unequal length wishbones, coil springs.
Steering: rack and pinion with power assistance.
Tyres: 19/20in according to model.
DIMENSIONS: **length**: 15ft 7.5in; **width**: 6ft 1in; **height**: 4ft 3in; **wheelbase**: 9ft; **track**: front 5ft 08in; rear 5ft 08in; **weight**: 3516lb (3.5/4.2), 3691lb (supercharged).

XKRs had the brightly finished front wing vents and larger wheels/tyres.

Contrast stitching and different woodwork for the first generation Portfolio.

The XK went on to be further developed through two face-lifts, until 2014, beyond the scope of this publication.

ALSO FROM VELOCE –

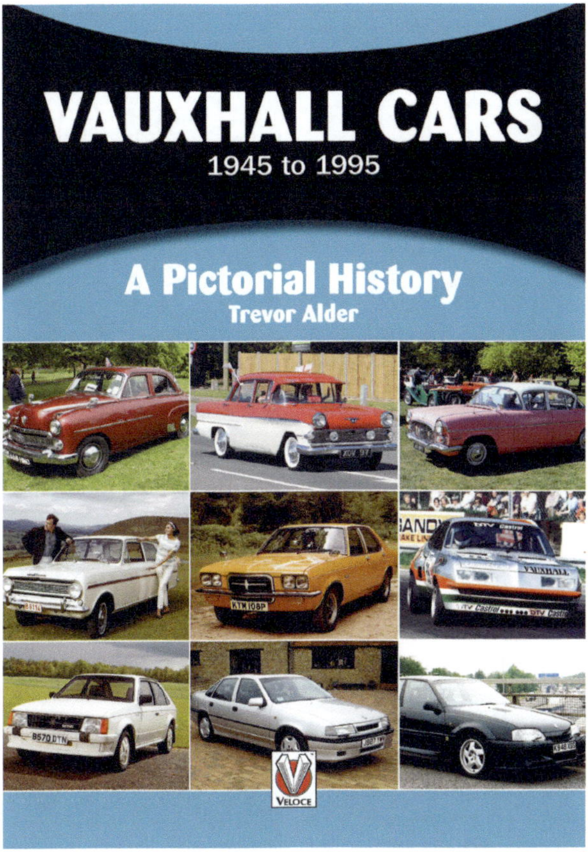

ISBN: 978-1-787115-93-4
Paperback • 21x14.8cm • 160 pages
• 340 colour pictures

Profusely illustrated throughout, a worthy addition to the Veloce Pictorial History series. Every Vauxhall model (1945-1995) has been painstakingly researched detailing body derivatives, production changes, technical information and hundreds of period photos and diagrams, plus how the ever-changing advertising was used to promote each model.

For more information and price details, visit our website at www.veloce.co.uk • email: info@veloce.co.uk • Tel: +44(0)1305 260068

ALSO FROM VELOCE –

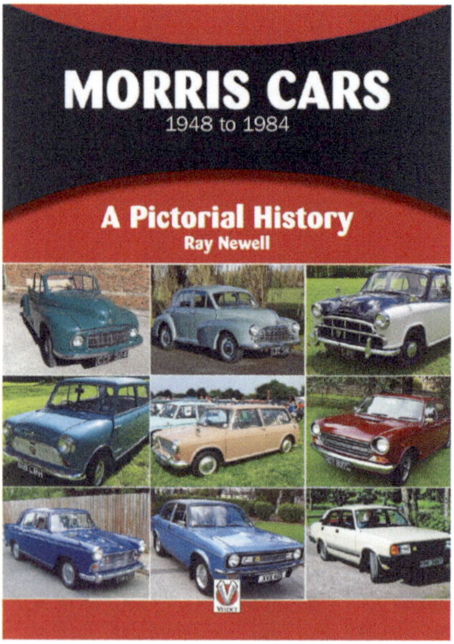

ISBN: 978-1-787110-55-7
Paperback • 21x14.8cm • 144 pages
• 425 colour pictures

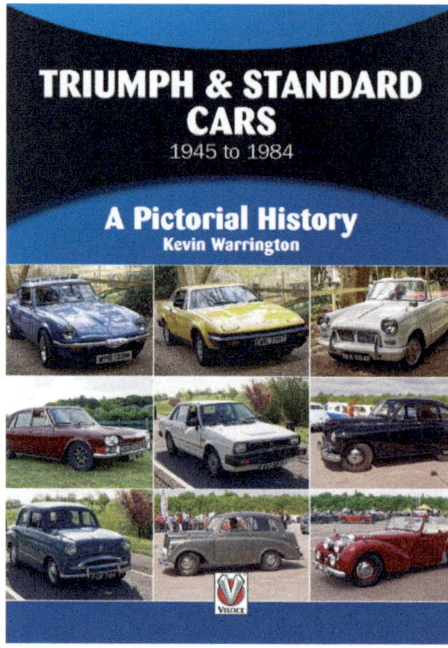

ISBN: 978-1-787110-77-9
Paperback • 21x14.8cm • 96 pages
• 244 colour pictures

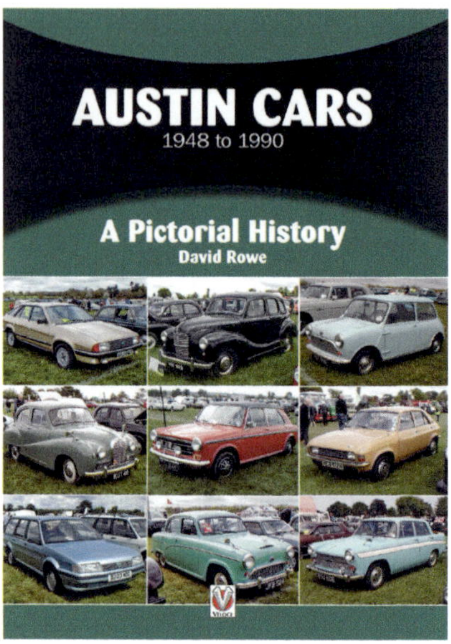

ISBN: 978-1-787112-19-3
Paperback • 21x14.8cm • 112 pages
• 275 colour and b&w pictures

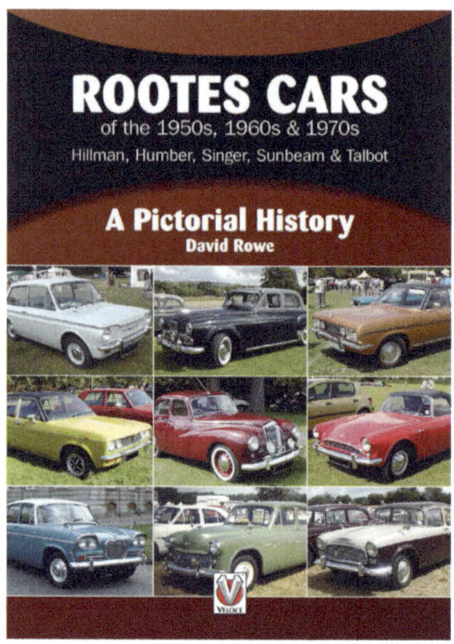

ISBN: 978-1-787114-43-2
Paperback • 21x14.8cm • 168 pages
• 1083 colour and b&w pictures

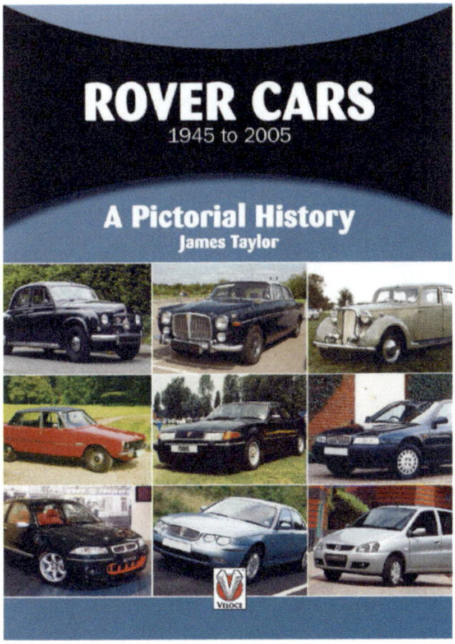

ISBN: 978-1-787116-09-2
Paperback • 21x14.8cm • 80 pages • 300 pictures

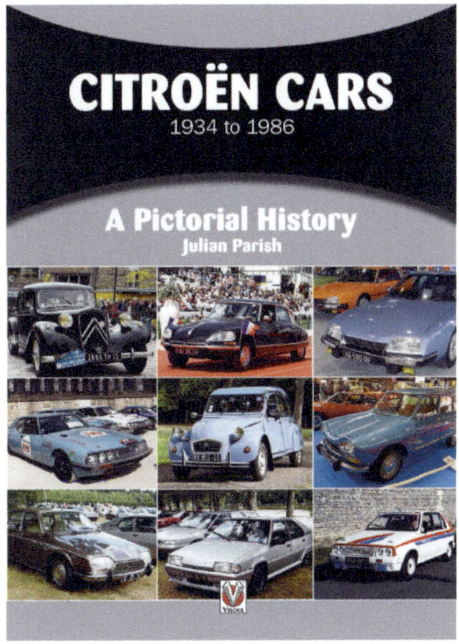

ISBN: 978-1-787116-36-8
Paperback • 21x14.8cm • 152 pages • 350 pictures

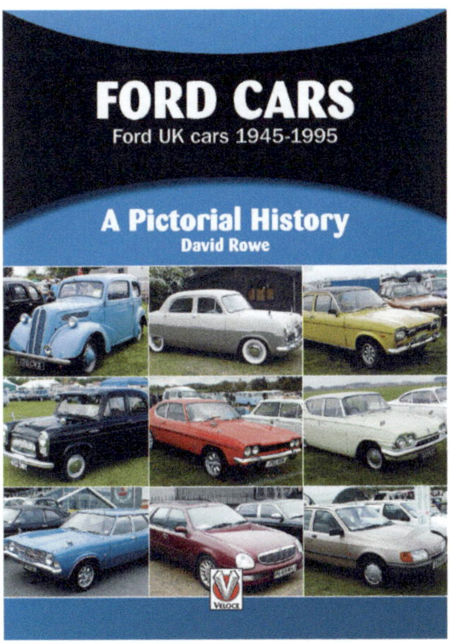

ISBN: 978-1-787116-42-9
Paperback • 21x14.8cm • 160 pages • 330 pictures

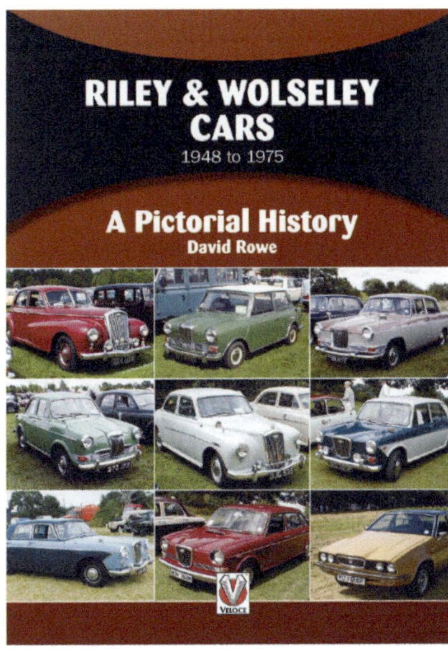

ISBN: 978-1-787117-91-4
Paperback • 21x14.8cm • 104 pages • 352 colour and b&w pictures

INDEX